Project Addiction Counselor

How to Create and Sustain a Private Practice

Scott A Spackey

RAS (Registered Addiction Specialist)

CATC (Certified Addiction Treatment Counselor)

CLC (Certified Life-Coach)

CHt (Certified Clinical Hypnotherapist)

Owner of LifeMind Counseling Centers

Project Addiction Counselor
How to Create and Sustain a Private Practice
By Scott Spackey

Published by: Primordial Productions
24303 Walnut St., Suite A
Valencia, CA 91321
Telephone: (661) 383-3182
Website: www.PrimordialProductions.net
E-mail: CCB@PrimordialProductions.net

Print: 978-0-9968913-1-8
EBook: 978-0-9968913-5-6
Audio: 978-0-9968913-6-3

Library of Congress Control Number: 2015953967

First Edition. Printed in the United States of America
10 9 8 7 6 5 4 3 2 1

Editor: Brandon Pi Bang

To every client who gave me the honor of guiding them,

The woman who tolerates my solipsism and the man who taught me how to drive—my son.

JSR

CONTENTS

1

WHY PRIVATE PRACTICE?

Why should you begin a private practice?

To change the world and make a great living.

Being a private-practice recovery counselor is a fulfilling career. You get to participate in the healing and transformative process of growth and change with individuals and their families. You get to make a difference and a contribution to humanity in your own small but significant way. You will also have the opportunity to make a lucrative living, enjoying the comforts money provides and the freedom of being a solo practitioner rather than having to work for a company or corporation. Self-employment is a dream for many, and private addiction counseling is a burgeoning market with longevity and staying power. The demand for any form of medicine or treatment never wanes: whether the economy is good or bad, the medical field always does well. In a bad economy, people may tighten their belts and go without vacations and luxuries, but they always try to put a priority on being well.

For the practitioner, private practice is a win--win, best-of-all-worlds scenario: clients get one on one effective counseling that can be unique and customized and you have a fulfilling, enjoyable career, the freedoms of owning your own business, and tremendous profit potential. I should know—I've done it.

I created a private addiction recovery and counseling practice, and within three years I was grossing $200,000 annually. I did this all with very little start-up money and without getting an expensive and time-consuming college degree. This is all explained in the "How I Did It" section, coming up.

Wanted: Private-Practice Addiction Counselors

Seven billion people populate the globe. Approximately 230 million of them (6 percent) have addiction issues. In the United States alone, there are 316 million people, and approximately 23 million (7 percent) of them have addiction issues. However, only 10 percent of those pursue treatment. Every year in the United States, 120,000 people die of addiction—that's 350 a day—despite the fact that there are over 14,500 specialized drug-treatment facilities in the United States.

Why are only 10 percent of addicts seeking treatment? The convenient conclusion is to assume that the twenty-one million *not* seeking treatment are in denial or unwilling to commit. But the more accurate proposal is that the majority of people with addiction issues do not have confidence in the current recovery industry, which has a success rate of less than 8 percent. Many people cannot find quality outpatient treatment that is customized and individual, and many others cannot afford the high cost of treatment from this $34-billion-a-year industry.

Those are staggering reasons for why private drug-counseling practice is a good idea: it's about time and long overdue. Addiction is becoming more socially recognized than ever before, taking on an almost trendy quality: sports and entertainment celebrities often seem to capitalize on the publicity of the stigma of addiction issues. Reality TV and social media are cultlike, and addiction and treatment are popularly featured. It's a blessing and a curse: the attention helps destigmatize addiction and the treatment of it, but it also popularizes them to the point of near trendiness. We should not shun addicts in our society, but neither should addiction be fashionable.

Addiction is more prolific than ever before, and the recovery industry is expected to grow by 31 percent between 2012 and 2022. It is a growing field of service.

After doing a fairly exhaustive Internet search for private-practice drug counselors in several states, I was able to locate only three: one in Seattle, one in Los Angeles, and my own (also in the LA area). I don't know about the others, but my schedule is always full. I provide private sessions every day of the week for ten hours a day, seeing between six and eight clients each weekday and two to four clients on Saturdays and some Sundays. I used to provide sessions *every* Sunday, but I could not expect to provide quality for such sensitive work without a day off. In good conscience I cannot turn away someone in need, and there are always people in need. I am sure there are more private-practice counselors out there, but they are obviously a minority; otherwise, an online search would reveal more.

A Win-Win Situation

The benefits of private practice for the counselor are rather obvious: work for yourself instead of a company or corporation, develop your own methods, and earn proportionate private-practice revenue instead of an hourly or salaried wage. The Bureau of Labor Statistics states that the median pay for addiction counselors in 2012 was $38,520 annually, or $18.52 hourly. The median addiction-counselor wage is barely double the minimum wage, yet the occupation takes training and skill and is highly stressful, as it comes with a tremendous responsibility. As a private counselor, I average $170,000 in annual revenue; in my banner year, I earned $220,000.

The benefit of private practice for those seeking treatment is that it offers private, discreet treatment that is specifically customized to the individual client. Private counseling can be customized to the person seeking treatment rather than requiring the client to adapt to the program. Very few addicts are actual candidates for inpatient treatment, and rehab often makes the condition worse, not better. Many of those who fail in residential treatment thrive and do very well in private outpatient counseling. I should know!

Many private-counseling clients realize more substantial and quicker results while saving tens of thousands of dollars. The average inpatient recovery facility cost ranges between $2,000 and $10,000 per week. Ninety-day commitment to residential (inpatient) treatment is the popular standard. However, its low success rate (less than 10 percent) means most participants need to return to treatment and thus incur additional costs. Some facilities offer a discounted rate for return patients, something like a frequent-buyer card. But most people cannot afford residential treatment even once, let alone twice, and most cannot disappear from their families or jobs for thirty to ninety days for treatment.

Alternatively, the average cost of private counseling ranges from $150 to $300 per week, depending on the frequency of sessions. Clients can participate in ninety days of intense, productive, and customized treatment for under $5,000. Treatment longevity is somewhat unique to private counseling. Establishing abstinence takes a bit longer, but once it has been established, it is more stable.

Treatment is the process by which we try to improve a defect. Addiction and its recovery are far too personal and unique to each individual to assume that any single process or treatment is good just the way it is for everyone. What may work well for one person at a facility may not work at all for another. A large facility program does not have the ability to adapt to individual patients; in fact, most treatment centers have a general program that requires patients to adapt to it, not the other way around.

Treatments need to be customized and modified to who we are, what we're doing, what we've done, and where we're going. General treatment philosophies are simply not workable, and anyone who suggests that one particular philosophy or program is universally adaptable "if done right" is revealing how ignorant he or she is about recovery. Believing that a program works perfectly and that its failure can only be the fault of the participant is passing the buck. My job as a counselor and mentor is to keep customizing and finding the formula that resonates with the individual who has reached out to me for help. Successful recovery is not about making clients conform to a strategy of mine; it is about creating a strategy that conforms to them. It is true that many recovery failures are the result of individuals who are not truly committed to recovery, but it is *my* job—as the professional—to recognize their limitations and to get them committed, which requires a different process of persuasion for each person I counsel.

Yes, there are universal truths and strategies for recovery, but details and nuances need to be tailored to the individual.

Outpatient counseling has distinct advantages over facility treatment:

- It can be customized to the individual.
- It is provided while the individual is living in the real world.
- It's considerably less expensive or intrusive to daily living.
  a. One need not leave his or her town, job, family, or life to get it.

Let's expand on these particulars (reprinted from *Project Addiction: The Complete Guide to Using, Abusing and Recovering from Addictive Drugs and Behaviors*):

Treatment is customized to the individual.
Advice can be tailored to the individual clients. What are they capable of? Are they ready to run a recovery marathon, or do they need to start with slow walking or even crawling? Are they spiritually minded? Religious? Antireligious? What kind of lives do they want for themselves? Are they deep thinkers or superficial thinkers? It's not your job to make them similar to you; it's your job to help them realize their own potential. A counselor's job is not to define happiness, but to help the

clients define it and attain it on their own terms and according to their own personalities.

Treatment is provided while the individual is living in the real world.
Residential treatment is insular. Outpatient treatment allows clients to learn as they go.

While the learning-as-you-go approach is riskier, the challenges it presents are the challenges all addicts must face someday to adapt to the world without drugs. An outpatient doesn't enjoy the immediate abstinence that a resident does, but in the long run, where it really counts, the outpatient enjoys the long-term sobriety that a resident does not. A personal counselor can help clients deal with probable scenarios by advising them in *real time*. Counselor and client can work together on specific stressors before, during, and after they occur. Potential problems such as pressure with school are anticipated, and strategies and solutions for specific dynamics are custom-built to work in real-life situations, not just in theory. A counselor can tell you how to deal not just with classes or girlfriends or boyfriends, but with *your* classes and *your* girlfriend or boyfriend.

Clients don't have to leave their town, job, family, or life to get it.
Many people cannot commit to a residential program because the thought of leaving everything they know is far too intimidating for them, even when everything they know is toxic and irritating. If clients have school, friends, jobs, romantic relationships, or family—anything they believe is important—they're not likely willing to leave it behind. Most addicts are in dire straits: they're broke and need to work. They may be in danger of losing their job or spouse. Leaving can make things worse in some ways, so they need a program they can do while earning a living, going to school, or keeping up their house or family. Moving into an inpatient facility is simply not an option for many.

It's considerably less expensive and intrusive.

If someone sees an outpatient counselor four times a month (once per week), the cost is between $500 and $800, including drug screens. Twelve months would cost from $7,000 to $10,000 maximum. Most clients need sessions biweekly or weekly for the first three months, every other week for the following three, and one to two times per month thereafter. They can always have more time if they need it or less if they don't. Not only is this less expensive than residential treatment, but also the amount is not due up front or in huge installments. Private counseling allows clients to pay as they go; this means they can come more often if treatment is needed and they can afford it—or less if it's not or they can't. The client and family decide what's best and affordable. A counselor should evaluate the client's need and make a recommendation, but he or she cannot force anything.

Outpatient treatment is less intrusive because clients, in general, come once per week. Additional meetings occur only if their schedules and budgets permit.

Fast-Food Recovery

Typically, outpatient treatment is best for most addicts, but finding a good counselor is challenging. Most counselors are swallowed up by residential facilities that underpay them and insist they conform to generic programs. The poor compensation counselors receive in this industry is a problem: smart and resourceful recovered addicts do not find counseling a lucrative option, so they don't turn to it. This creates a majority of counselors who are intellectually and emotionally underqualified and inexperienced in real-life addiction.

Addiction Counselors: Sherpas of Recovery

Counselors who are addicts (either recovered or recovering) are familiar with the territory of addiction: they have instincts and insights that nonaddict doctors and

7

clinicians do not have. Like a Sherpa, they've lived it: they've been there and done that.

Sherpas are Tibetan natives who can be hired to guide mountain climbers up the treacherous slopes of Mount Everest and other Himalayan mountains, like K2. They have lived there for generations and know the climate, the trails, the weather—the ins and outs of the region. Counselors with personal recovery experience have access to recovery perspectives that nonaddicts do not.

Outpatient treatment is appropriate for those with almost all degrees of addiction. The exception is the addict who is using so severely and frequently that permanent damage is imminent. When using is so reckless and dangerous as to bring about a life-threatening situation, residential treatment is a must.

Now, I know what you're thinking: anyone using drugs is in a potentially life-threatening situation. While that is technically true, the risk to a user who is smoking heroin, drinking heavily, or doing meth is typically not critical. Meth can't kill you. It can make you kill *yourself*, sure, but meth in and of itself is not deadly. Smoking heroin is dangerous, but it's extremely unlikely that someone will OD *smoking* smack. Drinking excessively is dangerous and can definitely be life threatening, especially considering the type of behaviors a drinker may exhibit while drunk (e.g., driving or fighting), but we can't be neurotic about it. We need to evaluate the risk and the actual threat of someone's using. Pulling the trigger too fast on residential treatment is a costly mistake, both to a patient's finances and to his or her long-term recovery. So, yes, everyone using is at risk, but saying that every user should be placed in residential treatment is like saying that everyone who drives on the freeway is at risk so none of us should drive. In the dangerous game of recovery, we are forced to take calculated and controlled risks to reach the ultimate goal. Rushing to the finish line often makes things worse.

8

Residential treatment is often used to export a problem that inevitably finds its way back.

The Time Is Now

The demand for private-practice addiction counselors exists and is growing exponentially. My hope is that our society will offer both options equally: residential treatment and private-practice counseling. Society is ready for this shift in the recovery field, and I predict that a time is approaching in which that section of the field will grow to meet this untapped demand. I have designed this book to instruct you—in detail—how to establish and sustain your own.

How This Book Works

Section Exercises: At the end of most chapters are assignments to use for hands-on learning, training, and applying what the section has covered. Additional assignments are available at the Project Addiction Counselor website.

Case Conferences: Each chapter contains excerpts from actual sessions and case examples from my practice. They are all real and are not even slightly embellished. More are available at the Project Addiction Counselor website: http://www.projectaddictioncounselor.net/.

The stats on abuse and recovery at the start of this chapter and throughout this book were acquired from various websites and literature sources, including :
National Council on Alcoholism and Drug Dependence.
National Institute on Drug Abuse (drugabuse.gov).
Ideas.time.com.
DailyFinance.com.

2

WHAT YOU NEED

The Nuts and Bolts of Starting a Private Recovery Practice

Commitment

Absolute commitment is required to begin a private addiction-recovery counseling practice. Personal interests, hobbies, and other responsibilities are going to need to be relegated to your spare time, if you have any spare time, while you establish your practice. These sacrifices will not be permanent, though: once your practice is stable, you will again be able to devote time to your personal interests. But for a private practice to succeed and become stable, it must be the priority. Not *a* priority—*the* priority.

It takes a minimum of three years for most businesses to become profitable and stable; this includes restaurants, offices, stores, and trades. Many require seven years. It is widely perceived that if a business is not stable after five to seven years, it is never going to be. The IRS requires a business to show profit in at least three of the last five years. If it does not, it is categorized as a hobby, and tax deductions cannot be applied. Profit is defined as acquired revenue in excess of operating expenses such as rent, utilities, and phone service.

This book can help your business become stable in under three years and help you prevent financial loss along the way. Ideally, you want to show profit every year, even the first, or at least break even. This book is designed to make that happen.

I've established three businesses in my life thus far. While it took each of them approximately three years to become stable and profitable, I did not experience any losses along

11

the way. Each business showed profit every year from its inception, though at times that revenue was barely enough to cover the expenses of the business and my own needs. I coordinated growth with profits to avoid failure from growing too fast, and eventually those profits far exceeded my needs and provided me with financial stability, security, and savings.

A business that grows too quickly will break down, unable to sustain itself. In fact, if growth is too fast or too slow, debt can be overwhelming, causing a business to fail in spite of its potential. Accounts receivable are always more delayed than accounts payable, so pacing is essential. Training, marketing, wardrobe, presentation, office rent, and furniture are expenses that need to be paced, and each of these is specifically addressed in subsequent sections.

Credentials

Credentials and training are legally required for an addiction counselor. Hypnotherapy, life coaching, consulting, and advising do not require legal certification or licensing; you're safe and ethical so long as you do not misrepresent your services or provide services requiring licensure. Education and training are needed by most people, regardless of instinctual talent or skill. Education and training also add essential credibility to your profession. Abbreviations look good after your name: having *PhD* or *MD* after a name lends automatic credibility to those professionals. But while a college degree is proof a person went through years of schooling, it is not verification of skill or talent. Initials after your name are mostly placebo; they give potential clients abstract assurance that you are "qualified."

With smart marketing and strong people skills, you can acquire the same perception. Many patients or clients have a delayed reaction to a credentialed professional's lack of skill or talent. The assumption that professionals know what they're doing is strong and can have a mildly neutralizing effect on one's common sense and judgment.

This is true in any profession. Every profession has providers who are not good at their jobs, but licensure provides a buffer.

But regardless of your education, if you are perceived as qualified, people will reach out to you. Once they do, as a nondegreed professional, you will have to work very hard to sustain that perception. You will need to earn trust and confidence. And once trust and confidence are earned, they must be maintained. As a culture, we have been conditioned to accept that people with legal credentials are qualified at what they do.

As a nondegreed professional, you will not have that default protection. Insurance companies are not filtering or driving clients to your practice. The only way a nondegreed counselor survives or thrives in today's medical culture of exclusiveness is by getting results. If you cost less and get results, you will thrive. If you're not a member of the big insurance industry, then the general population does not automatically consider you relevant. Scrutiny is vital, and everyone seeking help in medicine should be selective. Be ready and able to endure scrutiny and vetting.

This chapter summarizes the nuts and bolts required to begin: credibility (license, certification, and so on), office space, and marketing. Each of these essentials is broken down in detail in its respective section. There are also detailed instructions on how to access knowledge and gain acumen to be a talented counselor.

At the inception of this project, I went online and researched other books on creating a private practice. The few books on this subject are geared toward degreed professionals, and they all seem to miss the finer details, the seemingly simple aspects of the process. This book provides the nuts and bolts of establishing a practice and operating under the assumption that you know nothing about it. I didn't.

When I began, I knew absolutely nothing about how to begin a practice. I knew nothing about websites, business cards, marketing—I had never worked in an office a day in my life. I knew absolutely nothing about office life, let alone running one. I felt confident about being a good counselor; I just didn't know how to get (and sustain) clients or how to provide any form of helping service. I knew about construction contracting, which is about 180 degrees different from counseling. The only office I had ever worked in was the bedroom in my house, which I had converted into an office to do my construction paperwork!

I attained my construction contracting license in 1994. The school I'd attended taught me everything about construction, except one thing—how to get contracting jobs. Not until the day I got licensed did it occur to me that I had no clue how to actually get a job. Circumstances were similar as I became a legal counselor: I had the legal status to perform the work and the ability to provide the service, but I was never taught how to make a living at it.

Nuts before Bolts

There are countless certifications that may augment your practice or be of specific interest to you and the type of services you want to provide. While many of them may not have legal requirements for professional practice, it is advisable to train and receive certification for each, where possible. This book specifically addresses addiction counseling (which is specialized and requires legalization), life coaching, and hypnotherapy, the latter two being generalized and versatile modalities that can complement a recovery practice. Life coaching and hypnotherapy are not required to sustain an addiction-recovery practice, but they can be easy to attain skill in and can make your practice lucrative. Being lucrative is the difference between earning enough to make ends meet and generating enough profit to live comfortably and safely.

Addiction counseling may indeed sustain a full-time practice, but it may not. Other modalities (such as life coaching and hypnotherapy) can be used to sustain a full-time practice and yield the desired revenue to make it a lucrative career. Of these three, addiction counseling will provide the bulk of practice, but counseling alone is not always enough to sustain a satisfying income. Likewise, hypnotherapy and life-coaching services can provide nearly enough clientele to fill a full-time schedule, but they don't necessarily produce the desired income. Offering all three can mean working thirty sessions each week instead of twenty, which is a difference of about $130,000 a year. While I would love to only work twenty hours a week, I want security and comfort: $130,000 is a good living, but $200,000 is a very comfortable and secure one.

With these particular three services, it is likely that 60 percent of your services will be related to addiction, 30 percent will be life coaching, and the remaining 10 percent will be hypnotherapy. This, of course, will fluctuate. The three can overlap, as well, as it is often beneficial to synthesize all three modalities to serve a single client. Hypnotherapy and life coaching are addressed in this book for a specific reason: I can personally verify that they can and do work, and they dovetail nicely, complementing addiction counseling and each other. They can stand independently or enhance one another. I'm not insisting that these modalities are requirements for private-practice success. These are suggestions, nothing more.

Addiction-recovery counseling may be enough to sustain a private practice for you, but at this time, with today's recovery-industry empire (RIE), private-practice recovery is still considered an *alternative* by society, and the RIE spends billions to keep it that way.

Any alternative modality you like, prefer, believe in, are trained in, or want to add to your services may be enough to create and sustain an independent practice. Mix, match, and combine, as needed. You may offer yoga, energy healing, meditation, fitness training, and the like.

There are countless issues and behaviors that can be served by hypnotherapy and life coaching, and these services help to market each other. Once you begin providing hypnotherapy for clients, it will typically lead into other areas of their lives. Life-coaching services can then be fused into the sessions, as you advise clients in several life areas to triumph over a presenting issue. Likewise, providing life-coaching services can often lead to providing hypnotherapy. A few sessions can turn into a longer practice in a client's life, benefiting both your practice (with sustainability) as well as your clients (with progress and success).

For example, if a client comes to you to quit smoking and confesses that his smoking impulse is due to stress, it becomes beneficial to apply hypnotherapy for stress and to coach him on stress-reduction strategies. If a large source of his stress is a spouse or a child, it becomes essential to coach him on relationship or parenting strategies. Soon, you become a reliable source for several, maybe even all, of the client's life issues and challenges. If his source of stress is a friend or family member who is abusing drugs, food, sex, or anything addictive, your credential as an addiction specialist qualifies you to provide service for that issue as well. In many cases, you may become indispensable in a client's life. Hypnotherapy can lead to life coaching, which can lead to addiction counseling; addiction counseling can lead to life coaching, which can lead to hypnotherapy. The three intertwine and can generally apply to most people and situations. They are versatile. Let's review these modalities.

16

The Modalities

Addiction Counselor. This position requires legal certification or licensing which varies from state to state and each state (three to eighteen months training or education, which costs between $3000 and $5000). You will be required to be certified by the state you provide counseling in, since a state's certification is not transferable to another state. Each state has its own particular requirements, but they are similar. While you are required to pass a state's counseling exam to become legally certified, much, most, or all of your training and experience from another state can be applied toward certification if it meets or exceeds the minimum standards.

A drug counselor is authorized to have group sessions and to provide treatment. Treatment provided must be specific to addictive issues. If it is not, it can be perceived as therapy, and it is malpractice for you to provide therapy as a counselor. This may seem like semantics, but these details are significant. While a therapist can provide counseling, a counselor cannot provide therapy.

However, each and every bad habit or behavior that detracts from someone's life can be categorized as an addiction. They are all driven by the same mental, psychological, and neurochemical forces by varying magnitudes of impulse or compulsion. Many behaviors and issues qualify as addictive, providing a somewhat wide umbrella of protection and latitude for you to address many areas of someone's life. There are few behaviors and problems that are exempt from an addiction counselor's scope. The specific scope and boundaries are explained in detail in the addiction counseling chapter.

Certified Hypnotherapist (CHt). Licensing is not required for hypnotherapy because it is considered an "avocational" profession. Hypnotherapists provide a service, not treatment; treatment is out of their scope. Avocational help is not clinical treatment. To represent hypnotherapy as treatment would be fraud and malpractice. Hypnotherapists can consult, coach, or advise one person at a time only. If more than one person is present in the session, it is considered a group session, making it illegal for anyone but a degreed therapist to provide. However, this does not apply to a workshop or seminar event. Technically, a hypnotherapist can perform a workshop with two or more people in the room and provide service for a specific presenting issue and be within the law. The section on hypnotherapy covers the scope of the position and the legal limitations in detail, and also provides downloadable forms to use for legal protection. You must adhere to the law while providing as many services to as many people as possible.

Hypnotherapy clients may wish to quit smoking, lose weight, build confidence, improve performance at work or school or in sports, improve sexual performance, improve relationships, break habits, relieve insomnia, or deal with nail biting, hair pulling, or other compulsions. Hypnotherapy can be used for everything under the sun!

Each of these behaviors functions on similar mechanisms and principles as addictions, and a compulsive behavior qualifies as an addiction. Your addiction-treatment skills will enhance your hypnotherapy skills, and vice versa. Any habitual, compulsive behavior invokes your legal status as an addiction-counselor and allows latitude for services provided.

Certified Life Coach (CLC). Life coaching does not require a license and is also avocational, so the same limitations apply: a life coach cannot administer to groups or provide treatments. A life coach can advise, suggest, and recommend but can never prescribe or provide clinical treatments (or drugs). The term *clinical* is rather broad and vague, which makes it easy to navigate around, but it also makes you vulnerable to opportunists. You want to avoid legal entanglements. They are time-consuming, expensive, and distracting. Even if you win, you lose.

A life coach assists clients in building strategies to reach goals using a sensible formula. These strategies need to be customized to the person's abilities and comprehension. If someone wants to get fit and lose weight, the life coach cannot simply say, "Exercise more and eat less!" The life coach must advise the individual how to practice these wanted behaviors and how to adapt to them so they become habitual. Gradated plans and strategies are needed, and these can be enhanced with hypnotherapy. The sections on life coaching and the modalities elaborate on how this can be done.

Office

Having a professional place of business is essential. Once you are established and successful, you can operate from your beachfront mansion or in an alley, but until then no one will take you seriously if you are working from home. You've been warned, so if you ignore this advice, I will give you an advance "I told you so." The section entitled "Office" provides affordable, practical, sensible, and effective ideas to establish an office. An office is essential if you hope to be credible. There is no other way. Further, it is not possible to provide this intense service in an environment that is not dedicated to it.

Working Capital

It takes money to make money. This is a fact. I began a construction company in 1994 with $2,500 I'd borrowed from a girlfriend since I had no money of my own. I turned that $2,500 into a $300,000 annual profit within thirty-six months. Expect to have, beg, borrow, or steal about $6,000 to get a private practice open. If everything is done well and on time, you will get a return on that investment. If you miss a step, you may lose the small amount of capital you had and never get another chance, so be careful.

For the individuals I mentored, this $6,000 was more than they had, could access, or could even imagine getting their hands on. We were resourceful, and I helped them research opportunities to earn or borrow start-up money for their addiction-counseling training, such as student loans from banks, financial aid from the school, or family loans. The key here is to make training inexpensive—not cheap.

It costs between $20,000 and $150,000 to get a college degree, and while a degree is nearly a license to print money, it is not a guarantee. For many people (myself included), a college degree is not an option.

Not only was I unwilling to spend what resources I had on an education that did not guarantee success, but I also did not have three to six years to earn a degree and another three years to establish a practice. We need a fast track.

The needed $6,000 to $7,000 in working capital is for the following expenses:

- education, training, or certification ($4,000 to $5,000)
- office rent and furniture ($1,000)
- appearance and wardrobe ($250)
- marketing, including advertising, promotion, and the like ($500 to $1,000)

These are start-up costs. Once you buy a piece of office furniture, it is yours, as is your beginning wardrobe. However, marketing and rent are recurring costs. Your initial goal is to earn revenue equal to your recurring costs to neutralize them. In the beginning, if you're balancing zero each month, you're doing great. If your balance is negative, that's scary, and your days are numbered. By being conservative with expenses in the beginning, you can outlast the start-up time. For the first three to four months, your goal must be to generate enough revenue to absorb the ongoing costs of rent and marketing. A minimum of four clients per week is all you need to survive. This should net you between $300 and $500 per week, or $1,200 and $2,000 per month. Your monthly expenses—office, phone, and so on—should not exceed this by much or at all. Your personal expenses are a different story.

Tighten the belt in your personal life. With a lucrative, successful construction company, I was accustomed to a few days off, road-trip holidays once a month or so, and two or three bigger trips per year. All of this was in addition to providing for life's wants and needs and paying the bills. For several years, my construction business had earned me $300,000 annually, and I had grown accustomed to a comfortable lifestyle. Working both careers—my existing construction day job and my new private practice—required me to work more and harder yet earn less: I was earning 30 percent less in construction because I was taking on fewer projects to focus on my new practice, a practice that was barely covering its own expenses! I tightened the belt by taking fewer road trips and less time off. I took smaller trips only once every other month and made no plans for bigger trips or expenses. For three years I did without many things that had become familiar comforts. I poured my time, focus, and resources into my practice. I don't want to give the wrong impression.[1] When I began my practice, I was close to broke. Unforeseen financial issues and a plummeting construction industry had financially crippled me; my savings were nearly depleted before I even conceived of being a counselor. I created my practice, LifeMind, from and with nothing: no degree, little money, and no trust fund—nothing. This is why I'm qualified to write this guide. I'm not guessing what works—I'm the proof.

---

[1] I had rather humble beginnings. My father was a machinist and barely made enough to take care of family needs, and my mother did not work. College was not an option. I was on my own at sixteen and struggled to be self-sufficient and to survive my growing drug problem and criminal life. I'm well trained in going without much, and this turned out to be a distinct advantage when starting my businesses.

Don't Quit Your Day Job!

As hard and stressful as it may be, you need to work two jobs, establishing your new practice while working your day job, assuming you have one. If you don't have one, get one! The stress of working too much is better than the fear of not working enough. Overworking will stress you out, but this stress will be for something you believe in and can feel accomplished about. But if you quit your day job and risk everything on your practice, the fear of failure will impose itself on your work. To be good at the counselor role, you need to exemplify sacrifice, commitment, and confidence. If you are overwhelmed by financial fear and survival issues, you will not provide good service, and if you do not provide good service, you will fail. Financial *worry* is OK; financial *fear* is not! Overworking will feel overwhelming, and you will suffer, but there's only one thing I can think of that is worse than suffering: suffering for no reason!

I don't want to suffer, ever. But if I'm going to suffer, it better amount to something. Be willing to suffer and go without to change your life and others' lives. The experience of deprivation will fuse with your character and spirit, and your clients will sense it. They will be drawn to it and influenced by it. That which doesn't kill you truly does make you stronger. You cannot ask clients to do as you say, not as you do. You must lead and live by example. Make this practice your baby. We are all inspired by success stories, tales of those who persevere and triumph against the odds. Take chances, but take *smart* chances.

Now What?

If this overview has not disqualified you, then read on. Read each section. When you've read from front to back, set this book down and perform the exercises in each section. In two to three weeks, read this book again cover to cover. Continue with the exercises. In another two to three weeks, read it *again*. By the third or fourth read, you will become familiar with its content. Being familiar is better than remembering or studying. Familiar content becomes a part of our knowledge and understanding, whereas material that is studied and memorized is not retained for long.

Read and study this guide, and join the forum of others who are using this book to begin their own private practice. Ask questions and gather experience and data. File it in your brain, and keep building your internal database of useful information.

Become your own best expert. Let's change the helping spectrum!

Student Exercise
- Make a bullet point list of the needed ingredients to begin this career.
    - o Add one sentence ideas or possible solutions on how to acquire them
    - o Set these aside to address during specific chapters.

3

WHAT I DID

I do not have a college degree. I do not have a trust fund, a winning lottery ticket, or an inheritance. I do not have a benefactor or investors.

I am not lucky.

I am not magical.

I am resourceful and intelligent, and I have an ability to work hard and be tenacious.

I created a private-practice addiction-recovery and counseling office and within three years was grossing $200,000 annually as a solo practitioner. My private practice is still thriving. It is financially lucrative and personally fulfilling. I have the amazing honor of helping people transform their lives. It is truly the best of both worlds: profit and service!

I am not lucky.

I am not magical.

Here's how I did it. And if I can do it, so can you.

I've created two successful businesses in my life. I created both from nearly nothing and did not incur any risky debt to start them. Each business was independent, solvent and stable and provided me with six-figure incomes that ranged from $100,000 to $400,000, varying due to the economy and industry specifics. My first company was a commercial construction company and the second is

LifeMind, my private counseling practice, which earns between $150,000 and $200,000 each year.

I've included the story of creating my private practice in order to motivate and inspire you and show—by example—how you can do it, too. The practical information needed to create and sustain your own practice is detailed in this book. This section includes actual examples of how to be resourceful, committed, and tenacious.

Here's the brief version:

2005: Became disillusioned in my construction career and desperate to quit.
2006: Became a certified hypnotherapist.
- Sublet office space from a real-estate agent.
- Provided free workshops to promote my services.
- Worked my contractor job full time and saw clients afternoons, evenings, and weekends.
2007: Added life coaching to my services.
- Ceased contracting.
- Ceased subletting office space and secured my own office.
2008: Became a state-certified addiction counselor (six months of distance- learning training to qualify for state exam).
- Worked private sessions for fifty to sixty hours a week for two years.
2010–2013: Worked less (forty to fifty hours a week) but still tirelessly.
January 2013: Began writing *Project Addiction: The Complete Guide to Using, Abusing, and Recovering from Drugs and Behaviors*.
July 2013: Nearly killed in a motorcycle accident and revived by paramedics. Spent four months recovering, learning to walk and talk. Had to resurrect private practice and career while continuing with writing projects.

2014: Completed *Project Addiction*. Began *Project Addiction Counselor* while sustaining my private counseling practice. Worked on book on weekends and evenings for twenty hours a week.

Before the Beginning

I was a hard-core user of IV narcotics from the time I was seventeen until I was twenty-eight. I didn't graduate from high school or attend any college. While "normal" young adults were going to college for degrees or getting trained in a career field or working a job that could turn into a career, I was just getting by, providing for my basic needs through construction work and trying to manage my drug abuse.

When I finally resolved to quit drugs, I had a brand-new baby boy and all the responsibilities of any single parent. I had no support and no money saved. All I knew was how to hang drywall, frame office walls, and be a lying, cheating dope fiend.

Without a drug lifestyle to focus my energy and attention on, I found myself with a surplus of time and energy and a rapidly growing need to create security and safety for my new son and myself. In my first two years of sobriety, I took on more responsibilities at construction jobs to increase my weekly income and worked for various contractors, mainly hanging drywall and framing with steel studs. Sometimes I worked as a foreman or supervisor. The obvious trajectory for me was to attain a contractor's license in the drywall field. It was a catch-22. Commercial contractors need money, tools, accounts, trucks, equipment, and employees to start up; I had none of these things. Residential construction was where people with no resources began, taking small jobs they could do themselves and slowly building a business. But I would never survive there; I had zero experience in it. Things didn't look good: zero resources for commercial work and zero experience in residential work.

So I went for it.

I passed the contractor's exam (on my third try) and made cold calls to commercial contractors to beg for bidding opportunities. I drafted a cover letter, and on Sunday afternoons I faxed dozens of letters to construction offices throughout LA. This way, when the office staff arrived at work on Monday, my letters were waiting—waiting to be either thrown in the trash with other junk faxes or handed to the boss.

It took three years to build a client base, and in year four, I had three cash-cow jobs come in, netting me $300,000. I had no debt from loans or credit cards, and I didn't owe vendors or employees. Having solid working capital, I became a competitive player in Southern California's tenant improvement industry (TI).

I sustained my company for seven years, and each year was profitable, annually netting between $150,000 and $250,000.

Way before the Beginning

In 1994 I had a moment of objective truth, aka the moment of clarity, aka rock bottom.

I realized I could not live under the enslavement of drugs anymore. I had been slamming, smoking, and snorting meth for twelve years. I'd begun using different drugs when I was fourteen. I had neither hope nor belief—not even a suspicion—that a sober life would be a good life. I had no sense that being clean would be positive or provide happiness. Society said sobriety equaled happiness, but this was a conceptual theory to me. It was not practical, nor was it relatable. I had never lived a sober life.

I was convinced that my existence was a dark, bottomless well of despair. I could not imagine life being good. I accepted that being clean was no guarantee life would be good, but I fully realized that staying on dope was an absolute guarantee that life would bring misery and suffering.

My drug abuse and recovery are detailed in *A Stone's Throw: Memoir of a Dope Fiend.*[2] It was an agonizing time, and for over a solid year, it seemed I was in a black hole that not even light could penetrate or escape.

I spent ten years learning how to live without drugs, feeling the whole time like a visitor from another planet. I was not familiar with how to live clean or how to function in conventional society. I'd heard of it, sure, but I had no real or personal experience with it. I've heard of China and seen photos, too, and based on the evidence, I believe it exists, but I've never personally witnessed the place, and it would be hard to suddenly wake up there one day and live my life. Living a clean life was an abstract and alien concept to me.

Practice makes perfect, and over time I adapted to a clean life. Slowly it became familiar. As familiar as the criminal dope life had been, this new life was becoming what I knew. I was now a legitimate citizen of this new land called Soberville.

Along the way, someone who looked like me, sounded like me, and even had my exact name began a construction business that struggled for three years but eventually grossed a third of a million annually. Who was this guy? Oh—whoa—it was me. It was all real, but it seemed surreal.

I spent nine years raising my son and sustaining my construction business by building hotels, movie theatres, restaurants, and offices throughout LA. I bought an average house in the suburbs and had many relationships. Conventional (sober) life was easier than dope life! I was "normal." Eventually I met the girl I wanted to spend life with, and my son graduated from high school. Was this real? Lemme get this straight: I was not dead from a

---

[2] The memoir is a visceral account of the very secretive, sinister meth culture in the eighties and nineties in Los Angeles. My drug group was an organized cult of sex, counterfeit crime, and drug manufacturing, invention, and selling.

decade-plus of IV use of meth and heroin and prolific alcohol abuse, nor was I diseased from AIDS, hepatitis or some other disease transmitted by dirty needles or sex. I was a father, coaching youth baseball at the local park, and I was in a committed relationship with a beautiful, sweet girl. I went backpacking and scuba diving with my healthy, Adonis-like son. Who was this guy?

Even with all this, in typical addict fashion, I eventually felt discontent. I needed more, more, more. Sure, I was happy. But I did not feel fulfilled. My spirit was yearning for something I could not identify. Though I felt discontented, I could not identify what would make me feel whole.

The toxicity of the construction industry was wearing on me. All business is centered on the bottom line, and quality of work and character is low on the list, if on it at all. I was fed up with the developers and general contractors who promised fairness and proper payment so long as a company performed and delivered its jobs. I performed and delivered the jobs, yet the industry standard of creatively justified reasons to pay less than the contract amount—and thirty to ninety days late—was part of the culture. A payment that was ninety days late was actually a blessing since it was industry standard to pay at least five to nine months late. Lying and misleading was simply a part of the contracting business. It was assumed that if you asked to play this game, you were willing to accept the rules, and the rules were consistent: corruption, lies, and unfairness. When you go to the DMV, you expect long lines and senseless wastes of time and resources. That's the culture. It is what it is.

I needed out.

New Career, New Age

I began going to seminars and expos, searching for a new career avenue. I contemplated becoming the next New Age guru and sharing my years of intense work and study in Eastern thought, philosophy, and spirituality with humanity.

I saw a common feature among many of the New Age teachers, authors, and seminar leaders: many of them were also hypnotherapists (and many were kooks). It seemed like an essential part of the motivational leader's resume (the hypnotherapy, not the kookiness). So I looked into it.

I found a place called HMI near me in LA that offered a distance-learning course. All the training was presented on DVDs, and at the end of the program, I could become a certified clinical hypnotherapist.

I recall watching the first video course: I was on my feet, hollering with excitement at this curious power of hypnosis and what it could potentially do for people who were stuck in a behavior or mentality.

"I wanna do *that*!" I declared. "I want to be a part of the process of healing and transforming. I wanna *help*!"

Six months later, after working nearly around the clock, I completed the class and became a certified clinical hypnotherapist. The *clinical* label was a marketable tool, as it was harder to achieve, requiring more training and time. I could have legally labeled myself as such regardless, if I'd wanted, without breaching any laws, but I knew that being able to use the designation legitimately would add to my credibility. I could encourage potential clients to look into it, using those bragging rights to distinguish myself from other hypnotherapists.

I was ready. All I needed was a client...or two...or twenty-five.

Most of my life had been a matter of meeting survival needs and getting by. But since sobriety, I slowly became accustomed to my comfortable middle-class life of home and leisure, earning $200,000 to $300,000 annually from my construction business. I wanted a new career, to be sure, but I wasn't ready to go financially backward—back toward the life I'd had before I grew up and sobered up. I was now accustomed to the comforts of middle-class life, and I was afraid of losing them.

Who was gonna pay *me* for help? I was nobody. Why would anyone hire *me*? I was unknown and had no degrees. The only reputation I had was in construction, not in treatment.

Thankfully, I had some money saved up (not much) to spend on marketing, but how? Ads in the newspaper? Magazines? TV? Not only was marketing expensive, but what if it didn't work? I was at a crossroads: put up or shut up. It takes money to make money. What resources I had were limited, so I needed to be cautious and effective. So I invested in the only commodity I felt I could trust and was confident would work *hard* to protect me: me.

Marketing Action

I designed business cards on my PC and printed them at home. I carried them everywhere I went. I offered them to everyone I could without imposing, going for a soft sell rather than a hard sell. I created flyers promoting free hypnotherapy workshops and got permission to post them in local markets and other businesses. I designed an ad and placed it in two local magazines for $600.

(One time, I drafted one hundred index-sized cards that promoted smoking cessation through hypnotherapy. I visited my local drug stores and discreetly slipped the cards into the packages of nicotine gum and nicotine patches. Anyone who bought an antismoking product in my community was in possession of my card! Sadly, I got no clients from this.)

Quit smoking, lose weight, get fit, sleep better, build confidence—these were the services listed on my flyers. While I had workshop content, I had no place to offer the workshops. My garage was out of the question; a professional appearance is vital if one is to be taken seriously.

I would also need an actual office, instead of the spare bedroom in my home. I was so afraid I would attain clients and have nowhere to see them! I wasn't prepared to sign a six-month lease and pay high rent. I wasn't sure I would last one month, let alone six.

I saw a listing on Craigslist to sublet an office space near to me. A real-estate agent who was just getting started wanted to share the rent on an executive office for $300 a month. Tenants had access to the building's conference room, and it could be reserved a month in advance. The building was nice and professional, and the conference room was perfect for presenting workshops.

Every two weeks, I presented a different workshop. Attendance was variable: sometimes only four people showed up; I was lucky if eight people came to one. Out of those eight people, usually one would ask for a private session. It took six months to build up to a steady volume of six clients per week. One of them is with me even today. She was my very first client, and I have watched her transform over the years. I've been honored to have had a role in her growth and continuing evolution. She's been with me for eleven years.

Between workshops and my one small ad in a local magazine ad, I was seeing four to six people per week. I couldn't quit my day job yet: I still maintained my construction company, but my hypnotherapy practice was growing—and it was fun!

I dressed in jeans and boots to supervise my construction jobs every day. I then used my truck as a dressing room to change into slacks and a button-down shirt right in the parking lot of my hypnotherapy office building. I opted not to change in the executive restroom, as I didn't want to run into office neighbors or clients still in "construction man" clothes. I wanted to become identified as a professional hypnotherapist, not a part-time hypnotherapist/part-time construction worker, so I changed in the parking lot. I knew I had to walk and talk and look the part. I needed to fully adopt the hypnotherapist identity. Fake it til you make it.

Client sessions were slated to be an hour, and I found it challenging to fill the entire time on the issues presented, generally quitting -smoking or losing weight. I could interview a client and examine his or her issue within twenty minutes, and hypnosis took only another ten to administer. I intuited that people would feel shortchanged if treatment took only thirty minutes. People have expectations, and if those expectations are not fulfilled, they feel cheated.

To fill the hour, I would engage in conversation. It seemed natural to advise and coach clients on other areas of their lives that came up in those conversations. Most people are silently carrying a burden—an overwhelming responsibility, behavior, or concern—and are instinctively looking for help with it. When in the presence of someone they have confidence in and feel they can trust, they open up. As solutions and strategies became apparent to me, I shared them. Soon I was acting as much as a life coach as I was a hypnotherapist; in fact, the majority of session time was spent advising.

While we discussed smoking or diet habits, areas of clients' personal lives would come up and become relevant: "I eat when I'm stressed." "I smoke when I need to relax or my kids are stressing me out." These confessions were cues for me to elicit more details on these circumstances and to offer advice to remedy them.

Most smoking and weight-loss clients continued to see me after the presenting issue was resolved. Rapport, bonding, and confidence in my ability to properly advise them brought them back.

It was legal, fulfilling, and helpful, and it was beginning to be lucrative, too.

I added the title of life coach to my ads. Many people who called me were not interested in hypnotherapy at all and wanted to work with a life coach on life issues and unwanted behaviors. My client list doubled. I was up to about twelve a week, which was enough to quit my day job, but that quantity fluctuated. Some weeks I saw six clients; some weeks I saw as many as twelve. Each week, a client or two would need to miss due to costs or conflicts like a doctor's appointment or family obligation. I was worried. If I was to have a couple of slow weeks—or a slow month—I could lose my office or, worse, my house! It was a good client base, but I needed either better consistency, higher volume, or both to compensate for the varying client volume.

Eventually it seemed apparent that I had hit a limit: my methods were effective, my clients were devoted, and my reputation was gaining, yet the size of my practice seemed to stay the same. For every new client gained, one would reach his or her goals and move on. Some would quit because they didn't like the process (or me), and some would run out of resources to pay. My overall client quantity seemed to be fixed. It was a good business, but it wasn't enough to satisfy my material needs and security in the long run. I was a father, and kids only get more expensive as they get older. I did, too: as I matured and got accustomed to the sober life, I desired vacations and possessions. Both my son's needs and my own were growing.

My practice needed to grow.

Divine Intervention?

One evening I was watching an episode of *Intervention*, a show about intervening on drug addicts to persuade them to commit to recovery. It was powerful and inspiring and triggered a realization.

"Hey," I thought, "*I* help people, and *I'm* an addict. Hmm…what if I looked into becoming a recovery counselor and worked part time at a rehab facility along with running my hypnotherapy practice? It might not provide the income I made in construction, but I'd get by and be able to quit the construction business for good." I was willing to earn less in exchange for a career I liked; I wanted to be able to put the contracting business behind me.

I looked into the legal qualifications needed to provide addiction counseling. With extensive research, I found a training program that fit my needs: it was cheap and quick! It was a mere $3,000 for six months of training done in a distance-learning course. Upon completion I would qualify for California's state exam for addiction counseling. Distance learning was familiar territory, as I had completed the HMI course the same way and preferred to work from home, at my own pace.

I signed up and worked nearly around the clock again to complete the course. In addition to the course work, 160 hours of clinical supervision were required. So I volunteered as an intern at a local branch of the NCADD, the National Council on Alcohol and Drug Dependence, a federally funded and operated program. Within eight months, I had completed my needed intern hours, and I took the state exam. Now I was an RAS, a registered addiction specialist. I was legally qualified to provide addiction counseling in California.

When I began to search for counseling positions at facilities, I became frustrated and disillusioned. The rate of compensation was a joke! This so-called profession paid only nine to eleven dollars per hour for a difficult, demanding job.

I considered the situation. "I'm already paying rent on an office, running a monthly ad in a local magazine, and marketing through free workshops," I said to myself, "so why not offer addiction counseling as one of my services? I'll see if it flies, and maybe it will add the few clients I need to get by."

So I did.

I added addiction counseling to my list of services on my magazine ad and on my business cards, and I added addiction to my workshop topics.

Within two months I had a full client load and was working seven days a week for ten hours a day in back-to-back sessions. I went from having eight to twelve clients a week (approximately $1,200 a week) to having between twenty and twenty-five ($3,000 to $4,000 per week). Not only was this in the range of my construction salary, but I never had to wait three or four months to get paid. Most clients paid at time of service, giving me access to my earnings in real time.

There are a *lot* of people with addiction issues and a great number of justifiably paranoid, overwhelmed parents out there who need someone who is discreet and private to provide their kids with one-on-one counseling. A lot of people need something more customized than another meeting or group to go to. And a lot of people want to work with a recovered drug addict who is also an insightful, qualified professional who specializes in the area.

Within eight months of my becoming a registered addiction counselor, 70 percent of my clients came to me for substance-abuse issues, and 30 percent came for either life coaching or hypnotherapy or both.

That ratio was a blessing.

If 100 percent of clients had come for substance issues, I would have gone out of my mind! The work is intense, scary, and very demanding. You must be accessible around the clock. If someone reaches out in a dark moment and you're not there to talk him or her off the ledge, he or she may relapse. Relapse could be as harmless as a using episode, or it could result in jail time, eviction, or, worse, death by overdose.

Likewise, if 100 percent of my clients had come for hypnotherapy issues like weight loss or smoking, I would have gone out of my mind! While it is valuable work and it is an honor to participate in anyone's triumphs, eventually you burn out: smoking, weight loss, nervous tics, confidence building—any issue that gets presented day after day gets repetitive. I was proud to have become so skilled that helping with these issues had become easy for me, but these cases were becoming routine.

People seeking help are vulnerable, and they deserve someone who is engaged and passionate about them and their issues, not someone who is phoning in the job. A weight issue is anything but routine to the person struggling with it. It is serious and deserves enthusiastic attention, not rehearsed, generic responses.

These people trust us with their issues, and we are in a role of great responsibility.

As a counselor and life coach, one's level of responsibility is high and serious. Vulnerable people will often go along with anyone who is in a position of authority. Therefore, bad things can result if the advice provided is counterproductive or incorrect. Rounding your client load is good not only from a business perspective but also from a helping one. If you lose enthusiasm and passion to help, it will be subtly perceived. Helping professionals experience burnout: they become apathetic when the work feels routine and complacent. I've met many people desperate for help who were on the brink of giving up and living in suffering. After enlisting many professionals who could not (or *did* not) help them, they were on the brink of hopelessness. Their confidence was nearly gone; they were beginning to believe they would need to learn to live in suffering. This is heartbreaking. Clients need more than someone who is well trained and smart; they need someone who is passionate about the role of helping them and participating in their success.

Clients burn out, too. It is common for some clients to have trouble seeing you as a dynamic person in their lives once they become familiar and accustomed to your style, personality, and character. We need to keep ourselves fresh, and only by having a variety of clients and work can we sustain freshness. If a client seems to be getting burned out on me, I spread sessions further apart. Overall, it is up to you to be the dynamic force in the room: this means initiating challenging concepts and topics and also entertaining to some degree.

The average number of sessions for a patient who seeks help from a psychologist, psychiatrist, or therapist is six. That's average: some require more while others don't require that many, but overall, the average number of sessions a helping professional gets with a client is six. Because psychiatrists prescribe medications, they usually sustain more but do not have weekly visits. Many psychiatric patients only make appointments when it's time to refill their medications, which is typically every four to eight weeks. The majority of psychiatric patients are there for prescriptions, not for cognitive treatment. My practice was going to need either volume or repeat business.

For a nondegreed professional, volume is not the solution. You will need a combination of repeat business and volume. Volume refers to the sheer number of clientele you have over time. By getting a new client each week, you can have a high turnover: lose a client, gain a client. Repeat business refers to the clients who come regularly for long periods of time.

Fear is a Motivator

Allow the desire to help others and the fulfillment of a private-practice career to motivate you, but also be afraid. Allow your fear to motivate you. If you're not afraid, then stop here and get a job that does not require such personal and emotional investment. If you're not afraid, you're impractical and possibly in denial. In these circumstances it is normal and even healthy to be afraid of failure—of making someone worse or of being suffocated by the responsibilities.

I was terrified of failure the entire time my practice was being established. Failure was not an option to me, as I was even more terrified of spending my life in construction. I did not go fearlessly ahead, my fear of failure was greater than my fear of these new endeavors.

Be afraid. Fear is normal. If you're not afraid, you're lying to yourself. Be afraid, and don't label yourself as weak for being afraid. Be afraid and press on. Fear will keep you cautious, caution will keep you aware, and awareness will keep you smart. Fear is a virtue, and you should use it to your advantage. Don't let fear make the decisions, but let it influence them.

Go get 'em!

Student Exercise
- Make a list of any examples of my own story that could apply to you.
- Make a list of examples about yourself that have led you to consider counseling and private practice.

4

VISION

We all need a vision, an ideal, a set of principles and values we passionately believe in. Everything you accomplish in life requires effort. Your effort will be proportionate to the strength of your vision. When it comes to counseling, having vision enhances your skills as a counselor, and skill as a counselor enhances your vision.

Contemplate and meditate: what do you want to contribute as a counselor?

Imagine you have a magic wand that will give you one special power. You have the power to change one specific thing in the world, but it cannot be about you. What would you change?

Would you make the old young again? Allow the blind to see? Make the poor solvent? Allow the deaf to hear? You have one wish only, so you must use it wisely.

Which brand of suffering in the world would you eradicate with your wand?

That is your vision.

Meditate on this. Contemplate it until it makes you weep with empathy for those who are suffering. Let those tears become your fuel, and vow to try to make a difference. Vow that even if you never change the problem, you'll never stop trying. Know that you can never rest or be at peace until you participate in the alleviation of that suffering for someone, somewhere.

Let this vision evolve. Over time it will take on different expressions. Nurture it and care for it. Write it down, and every two to four weeks, look at it to see whether you still feel the same about it. If you do, then it's still your vision. If you don't, then it never was.

Let this vision statement gestate and settle for a few hours or days. Now, expand it into a paragraph—five or six sentences that truly express your vision. This vision statement has now become your mission statement.

Rewrite it, edit it, trim it, and add to it. Make it concise and perfect, keeping in mind that less is more.

Let this mission statement become your mantra. It should not be a slogan, but a condensed and distilled version of what you want to accomplish as a counselor.

Now go do it.

Student Exercise

- Create your vision statement or mission statement.
- Rewrite it at least every other day until you feel it is refined to what you want.

5

GETTING PAID

A counselor gets intimately involved with clients, making the business areas of the relationship awkward. This section will review some of the payment dynamics and provide tactful approaches to secure compensation for your services. Tact regarding payment can not only assure payment but also contribute to your ability to sustain client relationships and gain referrals.

Getting Paid

At the time of this writing, the average fee for a therapist, psychologist, or psychiatrist ranges from $150 to $200 per fifty-minute session. People always want more for less; therefore, it is recommended that you charge less, regardless of how much more effective you may be, and that you be more generous with time.

More

My sessions exceeded an hour soon after I began. With one-hour sessions, I found it too stressful to adhere to the time frame. Ending sessions in forty-five or fifty minutes seemed to interfere with both rapport and pace. It was so stressful to abbreviate important topics and needed work that I would consistently run over the allotted time. Making sessions between an hour and an hour and a quarter meant there was time to make conventional pleasantries when greeting a client without those pleasantries compromising session time. I typically allot seventy-five to ninety minutes per session to allow time to settle in and maintain an informal, conversational tone throughout. Some clients work at a quick pace, and some work at slower pace. Once I get a sense of what to expect,

I adjust the time accordingly. With clients who are conversationally conservative or not too articulate, it can be difficult to keep the session dynamic for a full hour. This is where my periphrastic quality saves the day—I am often circumlocutory. (I use more words than needed to express an idea! Go ahead—look 'em up: *periphrastic, circumlocution* and *sesquipedalian*—go 'head!) Others will run well past the time if I am not vigilant. A session time between seventy-five and ninety minutes allows me adequate time to be with a client and a few minutes between sessions to check messages, return a call, and have a small bite to eat. I personally do not take lunch breaks; I never have. I want and need to eat to be alert and continue, but I prefer to eat briefly and continue rather than go out or take time off, which requires me to work later in the office. This is not a recommendation, just a factoid. You need to discover your own pace and be sensitive to it.

For Less

When I began, I charged $75 for a session. Once I had a steady clientele, I raised my fee to $100, then to $115, and finally to $135. I was prepared to go to $150 per session in 2009, but the economy was struggling, and I wanted to sustain volume. As the economy struggled, it became harder to sustain long-term clients. Many would struggle to meet the expense. For many people, counseling is not considered a necessity, and it may be discontinued if their budget is tight. Whenever I raised my fees, the increase applied only to new clients, not existing ones. To this day, my first client is still with me, and she only pays the fee she began at. New clients get intake forms with my current rate, and existing clients stay with me for my service and because they respect that I never change the fee for them. My first client began with me when I was in a 150-square-foot office rented by the hour. She drove about twenty-five minutes to see me then. Today she sees me in my 500-square-foot corner office with a view and pays the same fee we started at. She drives just over an hour, and we see each other every other week, sometimes every week if she is going through particularly complicated issues.

Currently my fees have not been raised in four years, and I don't plan to raise them anytime soon. I seem to have established a successful rate, style, and formula, and since it isn't broken, I'm not fixing it.

Occasionally, clients may disclose upon arrival that they left the house without their wallet, purse, credit card, money, checkbook, or the like. If you have already booked the time and cannot recover it, then it is sensible to see them. The hour was set aside for this session, and it is best to follow through with it. While it is possible the person may be trying to take advantage of you, most of the time the error is sincere. If you pass it off as a trivial detail, you make an important impression: you are cooperative, understanding, trusting, and reliable, and your focus is on helping clients, not personal compensation. This impression creates appreciation as well as a subtle sense of obligation from the client. If he or she is the type to take advantage of you, nothing you could've said or done would have prevented this. Every business has risks, and this is one that will occasionally appear. With clients who are the type to consider taking advantage of you, your response will obligate them, making them conscious of their decision. Most people behave how they are expected to behave; you've given trust, so they will feel a need to fulfill that trust. Bad people are bad people, good people are good people, and both express what they are— eventually. Expect losses, and try to keep them to a minimum.

Barter

You may provide your services for clients in trade, especially if they are struggling to pay the fee. One of my clients had trouble paying, and I was not willing to terminate service to her due to an inability to pay. She offered a barter: five days at her time-share in Cancun to be traded for sessions. She provided me the cost information on the condo stay, and we did the math to provide the correct number of sessions for her, her kids, and her husband. While I was willing to work pro bono, it would have been rude to disrespect her willingness and her need to be accountable, which could have interfered with our sessions. I offered to work for free; she offered the barter, and I agreed. (Oh—and I really, really wanted to go to Cancun.) Currently, I see a twenty-five-year-old man for a venti misto from Starbucks, which he brings diligently to each session. We both know it is gratuitous, but he feels much better than he would doing nothing in appreciation of my time. The gesture and his hard work to benefit from our time are powerful compensation for me. While he is not—and never will be—obligated to me, you never know what opportunity may present itself: if he becomes a qualified provider in his chosen field, he'll be the first one I call if I ever need those services, and I feel confident his gratitude will manifest in his service.

Another client serviced my air-conditioning unit in exchange for sessions. These can be risky barters, because once the deal is made, it must be honored. If the man had done poor work, I would've had to cope with it, not complain, and hire another professional to redo the work. Remember, it is your responsibility to take the sacrifice, not the client's.

Sliding Scale

Clients may approach you about needing to cease sessions due to lack of funds. This can be awkward for a client. Such a confession shows that the client has a conscience and is likely being honest. An alternative to confessing this to you could have been accumulating a balance and then not paying, forcing you to pursue the client. Reward this honesty by requesting that such clients pay whatever they can afford. One paid me fifty dollars for a session, but I gave her forty-nine dollars back, as I knew she was struggling financially. She gave me what she could sincerely afford, and that was admirable. It also allowed her to keep her self-respect. But it was then *my* fifty

45

dollars, and I did what I wanted to do with it by donating it to her. Most people will respond honestly and appreciate your flexibility. Another woman gave me nothing for the two sessions following the agreement, and I assumed I would be providing to her son pro bono. However, she paid for the third session, and even gave a little extra toward the two unpaid.

You will also get clients who try to lowball you, requesting to pay less than what you are willing to accept. When this happens, be straightforward. Tell them the minimum amount you will accept, and do not expect any amount over that. Here's a script: "My regular fee is one hundred thirty-five dollars per session, but I'm willing to accept less for clients who are committed to their progress and can be somewhat flexible on schedule time. What do you think you can afford if we meet each week?" If the amount offered is not acceptable, state the minimum you will consider: "My full fee is one hundred thirty-five dollars, but I rarely accept less than seventy-five. Will that work?"

If you state the minimum up front to save time, you may negotiate yourself out of a higher amount. Try to get the client to disclose an amount first, and then make a counteroffer.

If you have a client or clients who are taking advantage of the "whatever you can afford" proposal, you can stop seeing them by telling them your schedule is too full. If they ask to work on a sliding scale or receive a discounted rate, tell them you're happy to offer such but that you may need to move their appointments from time to time to accommodate full-paying clients. Give sliding-scale clients slots that aren't considered prime-time, and ask them to be flexible in exchange for the discount. Such an exchange might sound like this:

"I'm happy to try to see you at our usual time, but I may need to offer it to a full-paying client to keep the rent paid. Hopefully we can work together on it. I may never need to move you and will try not to, but if you can try to be flexible, that makes me able to sustain my office and see discounted people." I've rarely actually needed to move a discounted client's time, but it helps to be able to.

When I see a client work hard and apply himself or herself to our work, I am more motivated to see him or her for less compensation. If a discounted rate is arranged, it can be diplomatic to close the topic with: "I'm glad we've come to an arrangement, and I want you to know that the amount of compensation I receive has no effect on my commitment and work. I do my best no matter what I am paid, and once an arrangement has been made, I never want a client to give it a second thought. We've made an agreement, so you should never feel you owe me any form of acknowledgement or apology. I will work hard for you. The best way to appreciate our work and a discounted fee is to work hard. Seeing you make progress will be the best compensation I can ever receive."

Once the details have been arranged and settled, cease conversation about your fee, and try not to think about it. It no longer has a place in the relationship, so put it out of your mind. Overall, your gross revenue will be fine. Many will pay the full fee, and many will not. Revenue is about averages. Retailers offer 50 percent discounts because they make full profit on other items. The sales draw in the customers, many of whom will buy nonsale items on their visit as well. Each and every client you serve makes it possible for you to have an office, a home, and a practice. Honor this, and work for everyone—all the time!

Never perform at a lower standard, regardless of compensation. Take pride in your work and your role, and never compromise quality. Once you take on the role of counselor, your commitment and effort cannot fluctuate according to payment. Fill the role. Once you have made a fee arrangement, put it entirely out of your mind and treat that client the same as you would any other client.

In my eleven years in practice, I've noticed an ironic trend: the clients who are the easiest to work with—those who listen well, participate at a high level, arrive on time and rarely to never cancel or reschedule—seem to pay in full. In contrast, the clients who are more problematic—those who miss appointments, frequently reschedule, and need more attention during off hours—are typically the ones who require reduced fees and often carry a balance owed. I have no theory about this; for all I know, it could be a coincidence. It is simply a trend I've observed. Every business has difficult, high-maintenance clients as well as easy, low-maintenance clients; and the percentage of both is consistent. What does it matter if it is a high-maintenance client who has a discount fee? I am putting the same amount of effort and time into my practice, so what does it matter whom it gets applied to? The gross quantity of time and effort and revenue is the same. Within a few sessions, I typically forget how much a client is paying. This is a symptom of being focused on clients rather than money. If you do a good job, the money will be there.

It is the full-paying clients who make it possible for me to provide services and help to those who cannot afford help without a discount, and I appreciate them. Occasionally I acknowledge this, telling them how grateful I am and how many people they are circumstantially helping. If every client paid a reduced fee, I would be out of business and unable to help anyone—including myself! It takes a village, so be grateful for them all—the high-maintenance clients who pay little and do little and the low-maintenance clients who do much and pay on time and in full.

Balance Due

It is best to communicate payment issues briefly and gently. Many clients will need to carry a balance, which should be expected. E-mails can be the best format for addressing this, and there are two formats for this:

1. Attach a current statement with a simple message, such as "Please see attached" or "Current statement attached." This is very impersonal and almost seems as if your accountant e-mailed it. (Statement/invoice templates are provided under "Getting Legal.")
2. Add a personal touch: "I've attached a current statement of your balance as a courtesy. Take a look at it when you can, and please advise me if you feel anything is in error. Also, a quick update: your son seems to be struggling with some anger, and I want you to know I'm helping him on some strategies for it." The personal touch deemphasizes the business side of things, but it also opens up dialogue and can be an inconvenience at times.

I recommend mixing it up: use a different style about every other correspondence. It may be best to use only the personal e-mails with some clients and the impersonal correspondence with others. Hone your filter to determine who's who.

Collection

There are a few options for forcing payment, and instructions for doing so are provided in the section entitled "Getting Legal."

Forms of Payment

Accepting checks, credit cards, and debit cards makes you significantly more accessible. Many people may consider rescheduling or canceling because they are currently light on cash. Some clients may be unable to come at all if you cannot take credit cards (or insurance) as payment.

Absolutely anyone can establish an account on PayPal these days, and once it is set up, you can accept credit-card and debit-card payments in your office via your tablet, phone app, or computer. This makes it easy for clients to pay, as they won't need a checkbook or cash at the time of service. Within minutes of someone making an online payment, you are notified by e-mail and can mark the session as paid on your scheduler. No bookkeeper or accountant needed!

I had PayPal for three years before I ever even looked at my account. When I finally did, I had a $20,000 balance! It was like winning the lottery! The fee per receipt is minimal—less than what is charged by banks or credit-card machines. It is advised not to bring up the finance charge, which is typically three to five dollars per transaction. The small amount you lose in transaction fees is more than made up for by the volume of business you're doing by avoiding cancellations and rescheduled appointments. When you don't mention the transaction fees, you give the impression of being focused on providing and serving, not being compensated for petty amounts. This impression is imperative to a helping professional. When you come to a client's mind, you want to be associated with offering help and being an ally. Do the work, and do a good job. The money will be there.

I have several clients who pay me exclusively through PayPal by credit card. A month's sessions will typically cost them about $600, and I lose about $90 in transaction fees. It is tempting to ask them to either pay by check or cash or pay an additional 7 percent to compensate for the transaction fee, but offering conveniences to clients comes at a cost. Overall, accepting different payment methods balances out in my favor, as I am not perceived as being petty. Further, each finance charge is a business expense and therefore a tax deduction.

Accepting Insurance

If you are a nondegreed professional, insurance companies consider you "alternative," which is code for, "Yeah, we're not paying for that!" The insurance industry's agenda is clear: administrators are instructed to look for reasons to deny claims because denying claims makes the insurance company more profitable. That's business. If a company can deny a claim, it will, plain and simple.[3]

There are many people who cannot (or will not) pay for helping services not covered by their insurance. This puts us nondegreed professionals at a distinct disadvantage. Degreed professionals get automatic business due to their relationship with insurance providers. It is a clever, exclusive club that protects and benefits both providers and carriers and is, to some degree, veiled by the impression of quality. Fortunately, many people who reach out to you will have already tried those modalities and seen little or no result, which is why they're considering an alternative. Many are already aware that their insurance does not cover so-called alternative services. The clientele you lose by not being covered by insurance is minimal and can be adequately compensated for by two factors: (1) full-fee clients and (2) volume.

1. Full-Fee Clients: Insurance companies negotiate costs with medical professionals. Most medical professionals have two sets of fees: cash and insurance. When you go to a doctor and pay cash, the visit may be $125. But if you are insured, the billed amount is $200. Same treatment, different rate. The insurance patient pays the deductible ($0 to $50), and the insurance provider pays a negotiated percentage of the overall fee. The doctor receives about the same amount either way: the insurance company has negotiated his $200 fee to $125, which is the same fee charged to the cash-paying patient. As a non-insurance-providing professional, you will not be dealing with the massive red tape of insurance billing procedures. Highly successful degreed professionals who specialize do not accept insurance, either. They don't need to. While accepting insurance creates client volume, it also creates volumes of paperwork, phone

---

[3] An episode of *60 Minutes* that aired on December 14, 2015, had a piece on the insurance industry's agenda and policies.

calls, and administrative tasks. It's no wonder doctors need staff!

2. Volume: By not dealing with insurance bureaucracies, you will be able to focus on your client's needs and the issues they see you about. This focus will allow you to be extra effective and attentive. With results comes reputation, and with reputation come referrals and return clients. Referrals combined with results bring client volume, which will compensate for the few lost to insurance providers.[4]

If you feel it is necessary to be an insurance-providing professional, you can contact the different carriers (there are hundreds) and ask them how to become a provider. They can legally carry anyone, but is unlikely you will become a lone exception to their policy standards. However, there are insurance providers that specialize in alternative care, such as Green Insurance. While I personally have not explored the opportunity, I recognize it as a possibility. I have been very fortunate: my schedule is so full that I cannot take more clients than I already have, and I have been full for years. If my schedule became slow and I needed to augment client volume, I would definitely explore the relationship with alternative health-care insurance carriers, which are gaining momentum.

Negatives into Positives

It is best to sensitively disclose that you do not accept insurance early in an initial conversation. There's no value in spending thirty minutes on the phone with a potential client who ends with, "Oh! You don't take insurance? Well, I can't afford out-of-pocket expenses. That's too bad. If that changes, let me know!" Many people will ask up front if you take insurance, and this is a potential

---

[4] Clients lost to insurance-providing professionals vary from area to area. The less financially stable or comfortable the community you practice in, the more clients you will lose to insurance-provider help.

indicator that if you do not, they cannot consider you. Handled properly, this can turn around (if they have the resources). Here's a script:

"Do you take insurance?"

"No. I do not take insurance as a form of payment, but I can provide you with the documents and codes that should qualify you to get reimbursed by your insurance provider. Every policy is different, so it's hard to say whether your insurance will cover our work together. An HMO policy will not compensate for my services. My own insurance is a PPO, and if I saw a professional such as myself, I could submit a claim form and get reimbursed for eighty percent of the fee. I don't know your policy's details, and since insurance is not my field, I cannot say for certain. About ninety percent of my clients with PPOs get reimbursed for what I provide. So you'd need to pay me out of pocket, and any reimbursement you receive would go right to you. I cannot guarantee it, but I will provide you with codes and take calls from them to answer questions and provide what they need if I can. I have deliberately chosen not to work with insurance companies. I don't want them telling me how to provide and care for clients, and if they pay, they set the rules. I like being able to do what I know will work for my clients, not for the insurance company. While you may need to go out of pocket with me, you pay as you go and can carry a balance. You can pay by credit or debit card, and you can quit anytime it gets too expensive. In our corporation-driven world, the best help is usually not easily accessible. Sadly, you get what you pay for."

This script is a template that should be adapted to your style and manner of speaking. With no degree or insurance affiliation, I have sustained $160,000 to $200,000 in annual revenue for eleven solid years. I wouldn't take insurance if the providers begged me! They're a colossal pain.

Work hard, work a lot, and de-emphasize the payment part of the relationship. Do not ignore it or neglect it; simply de-emphasize it. When clients have the impression that you are financially secure and that your practice does well, they conclude that you must be good at what you do, and this credibility adds to their follow-through on both the work and the payment.

Student Exercises
- Establish a PayPal or other account to receive credit/debit card payments
- Look into alternative insurance carrier/providers
- Research opening a business bank account

6

ETHICS

In any field or industry, breaking the law is punishable. In the helping industry, breaches of ethics can also be punishable by fines, suspension, or imprisonment. Ethics in the helping field are not mere opinions that are entirely open to interpretation. They are the recognized and accepted codes of conduct within the field. As a nondegreed professional, you have more latitude with ethics, but you are still vulnerable to lawsuits. As a licensed or certified provider of addiction counseling, you are accountable for adhering to ethical standards. The main standards that apply to all helping professionals are as follows:

- Confidentiality: You cannot disclose the content of any client sessions or conversations to anyone else without a signed release authorizing you to do so. The signed release must *specifically* name the people you can disclose to; "anyone," "my mom," "my family," or "my probation officer" is not specific enough. Without a name, you cannot disclose content to anyone. Verbal authorization is not legal authorization. Even if a judge or the police asks you for information, the most you can divulge is that you do see the individual in question. You are not legally permitted to acknowledge anything more; otherwise you are in violation of the Hughes Act or HIPPA. The Hughes Act is the federal statute that established confidentiality protection pertaining to addiction counseling. Degreed professionals are bound to confidentiality by HIPAA (The Health Insurance Portability and Accountability Act of 1996) as well. Anyone receiving treatment for substance abuse has the same confidentiality as anyone seeing a doctor (or lawyer) has. Unless the individual is a danger to himself or herself or others, anything discussed must be kept confidential.

- o If a person is potentially a danger to himself or others, confidentiality does not apply. You are required to report to proper authorities anytime someone is a possible danger to himself (suicide) or others (homicide, rape, assault, and so on). This significant issue is covered in "Getting Legal."

- Dual Relationships: A helping professional can never have any type of personal relationship with a client. A dual relationship is defined as any multiple roles between the client and counselor.

- o You cannot give medical advice that does not pertain to the presenting issue. (You can endorse a store or a product, but you cannot advise someone to use it. A friend can advise, but you cannot.) No areas are forbidden to discuss in general, but nonpresenting issues cannot be the focus of your session.

- o You cannot hire a client for any service, as this can compromise your role as a helping professional. The roles of counselor and client must be clear and consistent. Clients cannot babysit for you and vice versa; nor can they perform gardening, housekeeping, or other services.

- o You cannot have a personal friendship with a client. A personal friendship (e.g., going to the movies, having dinner, or hanging out) takes you out of the context of being a helping professional. This means that you should not provide professional service to family or friends, as it is not possible to remain objective, and this will likely complicate the personal part of the relationship as well.

o Finally, the big, bad mother of them all: sex. You *cannot* date a client. The moment your role shifts from a helping capacity to any other context, you are in breach of ethics and could face a career-ending lawsuit, especially if any type of sexual involvement occurs. If you choose to become socially involved with a client, you must terminate the professional relationship: stat! Currently, the law requires five years to pass before a mental-health professional and a patient can be involved sexually. There is significant latitude for a nondegreed professional, but that latitude is moot: under no circumstances should you become sexually or romantically involved with a client—ever![5] If you feel there are certain circumstances that could be an exception, then you're not ready for this field or profession.

When a client or a helping professional unconsciously or subconsciously redirects the other's role, it is called *transference*. Episodes of transference are inevitable. We cannot prevent them from occurring, but we must react to them professionally and ethically. A client may transfer feelings to his or her counselor. These feelings may be paternal, romantic, or of some other type. Likewise, a professional

---

[5] Any latitude that exists for a nondegreed professional is simply due to legislation's not mentioning or addressing a specific profession. Legal latitude is not deliberate. It is best to err on the side of caution in such situations.

may transfer feelings to his or her client as well. Below are several examples:

a) A twenty-five-year-old female with unresolved father issues may seek paternal validation by unconsciously transferring a male counselor into the father role, seeking validation denied in her youth.

b) A helping professional may transfer a young client into the child role to compensate for the lack of bonding in his or her own parent-child relationship.

c) The client or professional may feel romantically deprived in his or her personal relationships and transfer the other into this role.

The helping relationship is dynamic and intimate (i.e., close time is spent with people). Getting to know clients requires vulnerability, which is the genesis of transference. Rarely will anyone disclose transference feelings overtly. Transference is subtle, so you will need to have your instincts honed to perceive it.

If you find yourself having personal, out-of-context feelings for a client, you should not disclose these feelings. It is your duty not to confuse clients who are seeking your help and guidance. Mentioning or discussing such feelings is irresponsible. Transference is *your* issue to resolve, not the client's. You should recognize these feelings and assure yourself that it is natural to have them, but you must also recognize that they are not authentic and never—ever—act on them or even allude to them. They will pass either on their own or by terminating the relationship.

If a client discloses transference feelings for you, assure him or her that such feelings are normal and will pass, but if they don't, the helping relationship will need to be terminated. Never reply with, "Oh, I like you, too. And if things were different we would be great friends—or more! But that isn't possible, so let's forget about it." Never say, "I do find you very attractive, but...." Never acknowledge anything more than such a dynamic being common: "That's OK. It's normal. It's only a product of our work together. It's called transference. My role in your life is to help. It's a professional role that I am honored to have, and I would never compromise that role. I appreciate your honesty and am glad you disclosed your feelings. We have two choices: we can cease working together, for a while or permanently, or we can ignore it and give it time to pass." After two to four more sessions, ask the client whether he or she is still experiencing transference. Referring to it by its clinical name depersonalizes it, assisting in its evaporation. A client may acknowledge its passing or having passed. If you sense it has not, do not bring it up unless the hints given are overt. Maintaining your professional role in the client's life with consistency will typically make it evaporate. If it remains, termination and referral is the only option.

I have refused many invitations. A gay male client asked if we could have our sessions over lunch, which he would pay for, and he insisted it was only friendly. His suggestion seemed sensible, as he pointed out that the session would still be still productive but would be more enjoyable in the park or a restaurant booth. I replied in warm and friendly tones, "I appreciate that. However, it is imperative we meet here—in my office—to discuss your issues and resolving them. It is essential your mind does not confuse my role in your life. I care about you too much to compromise the trust you've given me to help you. It would be inappropriate and counterproductive to visit with each other out of context. Do you understand?" While my tone was friendly and warm, I was sure to be slightly clinical and formal, too. Afterward, I immediately returned to our usual informal tone. The message was clear, and I did not want the natural rapport we had built to be affected by this potentially awkward moment. I knew he felt somewhat rejected and embarrassed, so I moved quickly back to more relevant issues, making the transition seamless.

He tried to reassure me it would be OK to meet more socially, but I simply restated the same answer. After the third time, I said to him (still in a warm and friendly tone) that it was not possible in any way or for any reason, and if it was going to be an issue, we would have to terminate our relationship. I was cautious to avoid saying that he was making me feel uncomfortable or that his behavior was inappropriate. His behavior and curiosity was normal, and there was nothing inappropriate about it. It would be inappropriate for *me* to ask the same thing, but not him. He asked, "Would we be able to have lunch if the helping relationship were terminated?"

I was firm with my response: "No. This is the context of our relationship, and there can be no other."

Within two months the transference seemed to have dissipated. We continued to work together for a year and still stay in touch.

I've had clients offer me massages, yoga classes, construction work, and other services that I truly needed and are expensive to have done. Sometimes in casual parts of a session, we may disclose that our faucet at home is leaking or that our living room needs to be painted. This disclosure is normal. It would be unnatural to be entirely private about every aspect of your life. It is also normal for a client who can to offer assistance; it is common courtesy and convention. In each case, however, I hired an outside professional to do the job, politely offering to consider the client's offer: "Thank you. That's really cool for you to offer, and if I get stuck, I may take you up on that." Should the client inquire later if you still could use the help, the scripted answer is, "You know, so far, so good. Looks like it's getting resolved," after which you should transition into subjects about the client. Never should more than five sentences in a row be focused on you.

Clients may bring you gifts, which you can gracefully accept and appreciate, but you should not reciprocate. While your clients have one counselor to give a gift to, you may have several clients, so be conservative. Clients do not expect gifts from you any more than you expect a server at a restaurant to give you a tip for being a good customer: the customer tips—the server graciously accepts.

In my first year, several clients gave me holiday cards and gift baskets. I decided to place them on display in the office in order to enjoy them and show my gratitude: the next time the clients came in, they would see the gift they'd given me, proudly displayed. Then it occurred to me that other clients, seeing these on display, might feel obligated to give a gift to me also, so I did not display them anymore. Nothing but a sincere thank-you is required. A warm, sincere thank-you alluding to how much you like or will enjoy the gift is just right. Don't embarrass yourself or the client.

"Getting Legal" addresses specific legal parameters in detail and includes topics of payment and legal protection.

7

GETTING LEGAL

Each modality (addiction counseling, hypnotherapy, and life coaching) is addressed in its respective section, but here's an overview.

The helping profession has specific parameters that must be adhered to. Even if you are not a degreed, licensed professional you are not exempt from them. Rules, ethical standards and laws must be adhered to in order to avoid malpractice and lawsuits. Anyone who misrepresents himself or herself—intentionally or not—in a medical context is guilty of malpractice.

The helping profession makes you vulnerable by default: individuals who are mentally and emotionally compromised will be hiring you. You will need to be extra cautious in your practice to protect yourself.

"Ignorance of the law is no excuse" is a legal phrase, reminding us that you can, and will, be held accountable for violating the law, whether you knew the law or not. It is your responsibility to know your parameters.

There are currently no legal requirements to provide hypnotherapy or life-coaching services. Anyone can call himself or herself a life coach or a hypnotherapist and provide services. Life coaching and hypnotherapy are limited in their scope. Accepting payment for a service qualifies you as a professional. Advertising yourself and promoting yourself as a professional makes you accountable on a professional level. If you stay within the parameters of your profession and do not trespass into the territory of other professional services, you'll be fine. This section summarizes those parameters.

Legal Parameters

You cannot prescribe or provide medications or a diagnosis to anyone. Only practitioners who are licensed to write prescriptions may do so.[6] You should advise clients to never refer to you as a doctor or therapist[7]. Counselor, advisor, mentor, coach, or hypnotherapist is appropriate. Any other title could be misconstrued and bring legal complications.

With these three modalities, you can provide service to the entire spectrum of behavioral issues and disorders. While you are not legally required to refer medical issues to a medical doctor, psychiatrist, or therapist, it is recommended, especially with clinical disorders like OCD, ADD, and anorexia or bulimia. To protect yourself legally, it is advisable for clients with clinical issues to see you in conjunction with a licensed physician. If the client has a psychiatric disorder (e.g., schizophrenia) you should see him or her only by referral or once a waiver is signed by his or her medical doctor or psychiatrist. Information on waivers and how to use them is included at the end of this section and is downloadable from www.ProjectAddictionCounselor.net.

The legal forms provided here are templates and should be customized to your specific services. You should never meet in a professional capacity with anyone unless he or she has signed your intake forms. Many clients will arrive at their appointment without the forms, promising to get them to you later. Always have a set of blank forms in your office. Politely and respectfully, tell clients that you are required by law to have these forms read and signed before you begin. Tell them you'll be glad to wait while

---

[6] It is easier to list who cannot write prescriptions than the wide range of professionals who can. If you are licensed to do so, you know it, and if you don't know, it is a very safe assumption that you're not.
[7] This does not apply if you are one.

they fill them out (which will take approximately ten minutes), even adding more time onto their session gratis to allow for this.

No Diagnosis or Treatment

You cannot provide diagnosis or any form of medical treatment.

Diagnosis is the process of determining the cause of a problem or disease. You cannot provide a diagnosis for a client. You can acknowledge that symptoms and conditions may appear to be a disorder, but you cannot definitively label it as such. Wording is paramount. You cannot tell a client, "You have bipolar disorder," but you can say, "What you're describing sounds like the symptoms of bipolar disorder. Have you ever been diagnosed by a psychiatrist?" And you are permitted to have a dialogue about the disorder, educating and informing the client and allowing him or her to draw his or her own conclusions.

The client may respond, "So you think I may be bipolar?"

You may *not* answer yes or no. You *may* answer, "I'm not a doctor, but you do seem to qualify for many of the diagnostic criteria. You can do some studying on it or see a doctor for evaluation." And you can provide the client with reading materials about the disorder.

Clients may ask you for diagnosis codes for their insurance. Providing these codes is out of your scope. A client may promise to never acknowledge that you provided these codes, but you cannot afford to make an error here. On your billing statements or invoices, be sure to use the word *recommended* for diagnosis or procedure codes. Insurance adjustors may call or e-mail to confirm the code and explain that they cannot process the claim with the word *recommended* on it, asking you to resubmit the invoice without it. Do not do this. Advise clients to submit the codes verbally or on their claim forms.

Here's a script: "I'm not an insurance-providing professional, and those codes are copyrighted. If I write or submit them, I am in violation of copyright laws. It is legal for *you* to submit them, but I cannot. You can find the codes online—they're very accessible—but I cannot give them to you. Your insurance administrator needs to fill in a blank space on the computer screen before moving on to the next screen. As long as the code is authentic, it doesn't even matter what the code is. Giving them an authentic code, even verbally on the phone, is usually sufficient."

DSM: The Disorder Bible

Keep the *DSM-V* on hand. It is a good reference and a helpful text. The *DSM-V* (the fifth edition of the *Diagnostic and Statistical Manual of Mental Disorders*) is the so-called bible of the therapeutic community. It lists all of the currently categorized behavioral and psychiatric disorders and gives each a numerical code. The *DSM-V* provides descriptions of disorders and identifies the symptoms that qualify one for diagnosis. The medical field—hospitals, insurance companies, physicians—use the codes for their billing and documenting.

The *DSM-V* is an essential study for any counselor. You should be informed about the therapeutic and psychiatric community, and this is the reference tool used by all practitioners therein. You will likely get many clients a year who've been diagnosed with a behavior, and it is important that you are familiar with the clinical diagnosis criteria and can access them when relevant. The *DSM* provides actual diagnosis formulas, and if these are not met, a diagnosis does not qualify (i.e., three out of five listed symptoms in a determined time frame).

I personally believe in conservative diagnosis.

I have met many misdiagnosed individuals. ADD and bipolar disorder are the two most misdiagnosed disorders. Insurance companies require a *DSM-V* diagnosis to validate a claim and approve continued treatment. ADD and bipolar disorder are often used as catchall diagnoses. Seventy percent of clients I've met who were diagnosed by a doctor or psychiatrist did not fulfill all the diagnosis criteria.

You cannot go on record as disagreeing with a medical or psychiatric diagnosis, but you *can* have your opinion. While the medical field can (and usually will) prescribe medications, you are permitted to provide cognizant strategies to lessen, improve, or eliminate behaviors. This means you can work with these clients but cannot provide treatment (discussed below).

You are also permitted to provide verified medical data and information—how certain medications work, what they're prescribed for, and what the documented side effects are. Some of the data you use may be based upon your own interactions with actual clients. However, your scope is limited to sharing information and data. You cannot prescribe or discontinue a medication. You can share your opinion, but you should never redirect a client if doing so opposes a physician's or psychiatrist's recommendations. I recommend Drugs.com for information that covers the spectrum of a drug both in general layman's terms and detailed clinical terms.

No Prescriptions

You cannot prescribe any medications, and you certainly cannot provide any—*ever*. You can educate and inform clients and discuss the features of various medications. You may recommend nonprescription medications, such as supplements, but you must insist that your client checks with his or her doctor to be sure there are no contraindications (symptoms of toxic mixture) between the recommended supplements and any prescribed medications.

No Treatment

Treatment is the act of managing and applying medicines or surgery. Treatment is a clinical term, and you are not a clinician. You can assist, advise, and recommend, but you should never use the word *treatment* outside of addiction counseling, nor should you imply it. In addition, do not apply a formal treatment process if you understand it to be one.

No Group Sessions

Neither a life coach nor a hypnotherapist can have sessions consisting of more than one person. Services must be provided only to the individual seeking assistance, as you cannot provide group counseling or treatment. The moment you have a third adult person in the room during a session, you're breaking the law. You could get sued for malpractice since only a degreed or licensed professional can legally administer services to a group or family. If a client is a minor, you are permitted to provide hypnotherapy or life-coaching services with other family members in attendance. This is the only exception for those modalities (and is addressed in the "Working with Minors" section).

As an addiction counselor, you can counsel groups and families, so long as the content of the session is focused on addiction issues. Addiction issues and challenges affect every area of life: relationships, parenting, career, and health. You will need to discuss every area of life to address addiction. If someone insists he or she uses because of marriage issues, it is permissible to provide counsel to relationship issues and/or refer the client to a degreed professional. The central focus of the session must pertain to addiction, but there is a lot of latitude. Be prepared and willing to provide insights and advice on every area of life to treat addiction. Technically, if you spend an entire one-hour session discussing a client's sexual or childhood issues, your advice helps him or her improve, and this improvement is a catalyst to less frequent drug use or abstinence, you've remained in your scope.

No Dual Relationships

At no time and under no circumstances is a dual relationship permitted. This was thoroughly covered in "What You Need." Make it gospel!

Intake Forms

All clients must fill out and provide intake forms *prior* to their visit. If you provide service without having the forms signed (and a copy on file), you are at risk legally and financially. Intake forms are the small set of legal forms that outline your qualifications and limitations and the contractual agreement between you and a client. These forms are evidence that you know the law and abide by it. Templates of these forms have been provided in this book, and each comes with an explanation, in layman's terms, of its purpose.

DBA

It is advisable to have a business name (DBA, or "doing business as") on record. This is sensible for tax purposes as well as for legal protection. It costs nearly nothing to register a DBA with your local state or county. While the criteria are slightly different in each state, they are generally the same:

1. Download a DBA form or get one from your local county registrar.
2. Fill it out and return it with the appropriate registration fee (twenty to sixty dollars).
3. Publish a DBA notice in any local print publication (every town has one) for approximately four weeks (approximately twenty-five dollars).

Once your county registrar has provided you with formal DBA status, you can open a bank account under this name and accept fees paid to your practice, rather than to you as an individual. This gives limited protection in a civil matter such as a lawsuit. With a DBA, your personal assets are somewhat protected. It is not necessary to become an LLC (limited liability company) or a legal corporation. When you achieve enough success and revenue that such a status would benefit you, you will know, at which point you can look into it. Until your practice is highly diversified and grosses a consistent six figures, it is not a relevant issue. At that time, you will have forgotten all about this book and how you came from very humble beginnings!

Even after twelve years of private practice and $150,000 to $200,000 a year, I have not become incorporated. The benefits are not worth the hassles. My construction company remained a sole proprietorship even after ten years and $300,000 in annual revenue. Being a sole proprietor never limited me. If it ever does, I'll change my status.

Keep up on current trends and changing laws. It is your duty to protect yourself and your clients. I became a registered addiction specialist (RAS) in California in 2008. In 2014, the law was changed, and the RAS was done away with. RAS was absorbed by CATC—certified addiction-treatment counselor—in California. As an existing RAS, my current certification is commuted to the CATC status when I renew in 2016. Typically, old certifications and statuses are grandfathered into new ones. The new CATC requires additional education hours and other criteria and is more expensive. Sound confusing? Well, it is, and the details and process are described in the section on addiction counseling.

The addiction-treatment field is becoming more lucrative and is growing in volume. Sadly, it is a growing industry that needs more boots on the ground.

As the treatment field becomes more recognized and lucrative, there will be more government policies and regulations. The more legitimized a field becomes, the more regulation is needed. This becomes a blessing and a curse: salaries go up, but there are more requirements to meet to be a legal provider. Get in now, as this field will become oversaturated in time.

What is most important is to stay within the law. The five intake forms I have relied on for twelve years are included here as templates and guides. They are simple and minimal, and each form is accompanied by brief but specific instructions. You may consider having more forms, but do not have fewer.

Someday, life coaching and hypnotherapy may become fields regulated by state governments, too. Keep your eye on those trends and changing laws so you remain current with legal requirements and standards. The American Hypnosis Association (AHA) has fought hard to keep hypnotherapy out of the hands of government regulators in an attempt to preserve its accessibility and functionality. When and if these two professions (hypnotherapy and life coaching) become government legislated, they will likely become bogged down by bureaucratic complexities, diminishing their efficacy and dissuading potential practitioners from pursuing them.

Malpractice Insurance

It is very important to carry malpractice insurance. While it is unlikely that you will ever need it and you are not legally required to carry it, it can be an inexpensive safety net. The cost is approximately $130 for a two-year policy for a $200,000/$600,000 coverage. The first figure is per occurrence, and the second one is the annual maximum liability. In other words, if someone successfully sued you for malpractice and was awarded $200,001 you would pay $1; the insurance would pay the rest. The annual aggregate is the maximum protection you would get in a calendar year. Honestly, if you're getting a quantity of suits that even comes close to that amount, you're doing something wrong and should choose a new career.

American Professional Agency is affordable and easy to establish; it is the malpractice/liability insurance I've used since I began. I have never needed to invoke it, so I cannot elaborate on its efficacy.

Legal Service

It is also highly recommended that you join a legal subscription service, such as LegalShield or Prepaid Legal. For a monthly subscription fee of approximately twenty-five dollars (in addition to an initial setup fee of seventy dollars), you get access to limited legal help. I have been a member of Prepaid Legal since my contractor days, and the annual total of monthly membership dues easily pays for itself. Within twenty-four hours of placing a call, you will be contacted by a lawyer trained in the particular issue you have called for and provided with basic advice.

If you provide the service with the name, address, and relevant details (such as balance owed), the attorney service will draft a collection letter and mail it to the client. The collection letter is written on the attorney's letterhead and is in legalese, making it look formal and authentic. The letter of demand states the amount due for counseling services provided, requests it to be paid, and closes by stating that failure to pay the amount due may result in legal action. Payment methods and instructions are included. Ninety percent of overdue, negligent clients are intimidated by such a document and send payment very quickly. As previously mentioned, I will not sue anyone for less than $2,500 owed to me, but with this service almost everyone pays.

I have also used the service for a myriad of other issues, concerns, and curiosities, both personal and professional. Prepaid Legal also drafts your will with membership. If representation is required, you get a discounted rate and retainer fee if you use their lawyers. I do not need or want the expense of having a private attorney on retainer, so this is a great feature. I strongly advise all private-practice professionals to use one of these services. Consider it legal insurance with an annual $300 premium. It's better to have it and never need it than to need it and not have it.

Getting Paid Revisited

You may eventually have to confront the very awkward and uncomfortable challenge of collecting payment. If a client refuses to pay you, there are options:

1. Let it go. If the amount is less than $2,000, you may want to let it go, regardless of how justified it is to force payment. This is elaborated on later in this section.
2. Report to credit bureaus. Once a debt is on someone's credit report, the individual will need to pay you to have it removed to protect his or her credit rating. To report to the major credit agencies (Experian, TransUnion, and Equifax), you must either belong to them or hire an outside contractor. The costs and administrative work is rarely worth membership. Be smart, and keep your exposure to loss at a minimum. It will be more economical than being involved with credit bureaus.
3. File a small claims suit. Anyone can file a small-claims suit in his or her state. There are varying requirements to meet, and most are similar. You need (1) the name and address of the nonpaying client, (2) the date and location of the transaction (appointment times and your office address), (3) the filing fee (approximately $100), (4) time to file and to appear in court, and (5) proof that you have made attempts to collect and have been ignored (e.g., you have spoken to the client or sent a letter). It is unadvisable to seek payment through small-claims court for anything less than $800 to $1,000, as a claim may cost you that amount in time and aggravation, both of which affect your practice duties. Once a small claim is filed, you

are required to have the respondent served. Anyone who isn't you can serve the notice:

a. Sheriff: A local sheriff is required to provide service of court appearance for a fee (approximately fifty dollars).

b. Another party: You can have a friend, or anyone who is not involved with the case, serve the Notice to Appear to the client.

Once the service is complete, you need to have the Proof of Service form filled out to present to the court at the hearing (not before).

When you arrive in court, you will need to provide what evidence you have to support your claim of debt: copies of the client's intake forms and copies of your schedule with his or her name printed on it at the claimed dates will be your evidence. Also, save any voicemail recordings you have of their canceling or acknowledging appointments and payments. If these dialogues took place either in person or on the phone, document them: "On or about Tuesday, June 19, 2014, Mr. Jane phoned me to apologize for missing his appointment and the balance due of one thousand dollars. He stated he would be paying it in full by July. I've never received any correspondence from Mr. Jane regarding his having any conflict with the balance due or my fees. He has had the opportunity to bring concerns to my attention and has not done so. Since he has not refuted the debt, he must feel it is appropriate."

If the client does not show up to court and you can show the Proof of Service form, which proves the client knew of the court date, you win. Judgment will be awarded to you, and then you will need to collect.

If the client does show up and argues the amount, denies ever seeing you, or fabricates some account of your releasing him or her of the debt, simply state this is incorrect and that it never happened. The reason you're in small claims is to collect a justified debt. You would not waste your valuable time or the court's or Mr. Jane's for no reason.

Keep your presentation simple and short: dates, times, and the intake form are all you need to establish the evidence.

If the client says you were horrible and made his or her life worse, and do not deserve to paid, let the intake forms do your talking for you: the Acknowledgement of Services form, signed by the client, states clearly that you do not guarantee success.

If you prevail in small-claims court, you still need to collect the debt. You will either enter into an arrangement for payment with the court's assistance, or the client will pay on the spot (which is rare). If the client promises to fulfill the judgment and pay the debt but doesn't, you may have to return to small-claims court again to enforce the judgment.

An alternative to small-claims court is to go to the sheriff and force collection. The sheriff is compelled to uphold the judgment and will either collect the debt in money or confiscate property—like a car—and have it signed over to you as the owner. This process is not easy or pleasant. This is why my personal policy is not to go to court for anything less than $2,000. It is not worth my time or the frustration. I am not trying to change the world one person at a time through legal process. I am a counselor, not a lawyer. It is often more economical to take the loss. By following the attitudes and policies set in this book, you will be exposed to minimal loss. Never sue on principle!

Once a client's balance due is more than you are willing to tolerate, cease service to him or her; cut your losses and move on. Determine a bottom-line amount for your practice, and let that guide you: once a balance of X dollars has been exceeded, terminate service. For me that's about $600, but this amount varies per client. I have a client whose balance owed is $1,200, and it has been for over five months. They have been clients for over a year and have always been honest and eventually paid off balances (the mother even caught an error on one of my statements that was $250 in their favor, which she pointed out to me.) However, I ceased seeing a different client I had known only a month with a $550 balance. He never acknowledged the balance in any way—no apology or appreciation for carrying it—which is indicative of character. I inquired about the balance due in a few e-mails but received no reply, and he neglected to address the balance due during our sessions as well. My schedule got full, and I've not received payment or contact. I cut my losses.

In eleven years I've been to small-claims court three times over unpaid balances. The first time was a woman who owed $575 for unpaid sessions. We arrived in court on the scheduled day, and just before we entered, she approached me and asked if I would cancel the claim if she paid me right then—by check, in the parking lot. I agreed not to sign in for attendance in the courtroom, and once the check cleared, I would retract the filing, saying it was satisfied: easy win. The check cleared, and I followed through.

Another time a man showed up and stated to the commissioner that he had not scheduled the appointments in question and argued the amounts and details. Seeing the client-agreement contract and the copies of my schedule, the judge felt I was credible and awarded me. I received $100 payments each month until the $1,700 was paid.

One woman called me after she was served notice and threatened to allege sexual misconduct and bring criminal charges. My natural instinct is to seek justice and be resistant to anyone trying to take advantage of me, so I was willing—even anxious—to duke it out with her in court. However, my girlfriend made a logical point: even if there were only a 10 percent chance of losing, would it be worth risking my career, reputation, and all the help I could provide to others for years to come? The woman was clearly disordered, and maybe I should just let it go. Letting it go was counter to my rebellious need for justice. It took me a week to calm down, see the bigger picture, and recognize the priority: my practice and the work I did each day for those who counted on me were more valuable than proving a point. It seemed more sensible to remain clearheaded and dedicate time to earning the amount lost than to prove to anyone in the world that I was right. I know I made the right decision. We should never be so fragile that we require the world's validation that we are good, helpful, ethical, or right! You either are or you're not, and there will always be those who think otherwise. Always.

Terminate Service

If you feel a client is financially unreliable or not to be trusted, you may need to terminate service. A soft approach is to become unavailable to them, stating that you have a full schedule or a family obligation and that you will try to schedule with them soon. When you don't initiate rescheduling or respond to their communications, they will get the hint, but at least you did this sensitively and professionally. There's no need to embarrass anyone. Remind people of their balance once or twice, and if that does not get the response you feel is appropriate, decide to terminate or take the risk of continuing. If you take the risk, be sure it isn't so substantial that you cannot absorb it. In the beginning, you will be exposed to great risk. Eventually, you will get a reputation for being professional and established. With a strong reputation, you can be more assertive, but not before then. I've probably lost $3,000 to $5,000 over fifteen years due to nonpayment, poor invoicing, or invoice errors (I do my own billing). My losses have been far outweighed by profits, and profits have been attained by giving attention to results with clients far more above collecting. If you allow a client to run a large tab, accept that you may get taken advantage of, and ask yourself if it is worth it. Is it a loss you can withstand? One man had about $1,200 in unpaid sessions and continued to let the fees accumulate. Each week and month, he had new reasons as to why he could not pay what was due. He would occasionally pay a small part of the balance—a hundred dollars or so—which gave me mild confidence that he would keep his obligation over time. I felt dedicated to both of his daughters, who relied on me to help them. I could not, with a clear conscience, deprive them of the help they needed because their father was dishonest. (Yep, he was *dishonest*. He did not have some unforeseen bad luck; he just took advantage.) And if I had to do it all again, even knowing the results, I would. I did my job, and this job is not serving drinks or answering phones; it is carrying a tremendous responsibility—one that people trust. And I refuse to betray that trust. Well…maybe for $10,000, but not for $1,200!

Client Files and Records

All files, notes, and records you attain for a client must be kept confidential. It is important to have files and documents pertaining to clients, and it is just as important to protect this information. The minimum you will have on file for a client is the intake forms you provided to him or her. These documents contain private information such as the client's address and phone number and possibly a brief declaration of his or her presenting issue. Remember that the only information you are obligated to provide to any outside party is that an individual is indeed your client and that you do see him or her. If the only service you provide is drug counseling, then it is rather obvious what you are seeing the client for; however, a client may be seeing you for a friend's or family member's drug issues.

Also, while someone may be seeing you for drug counseling, the sessions are not necessarily for anything more than education. The point here is that you want to avoid leaving any type of trail regarding someone's drug abuse or pathology, as it could be used against the client in court or in his or her career or job.

I recommend using a very simple, minimal filing and record-maintenance system. Many organizations and professionals get bogged down by administrative details, and this can distract from the true work at hand: helping someone improve through counseling.

I will explain my own filing system simply to cover the basics and provide a basic template. I am not a great administrator; I do not like clerical work and do not have a knack for it. I rationalize this by telling myself I am placing focus on client needs. My success rate is high, my office is nice, and my appearance is pretty good, but my filing and clerical skills are merely adequate. However, my system has served me well for eleven years with no issues, so I don't feel motivated to change it, even though a clerical expert would probably be able to quickly point out the benefits of a better system and vastly improve it.

For your perusal, I've outlined my system below:

I have two large, wide, three-ring binders, a three-hole punch, staples, and paper clips. The binder contains alphabetized sections, and each client's intake forms and other pertinent documents are placed in the appropriate section. I use first names to alphabetize. I do not address clients by their last names, so it is simply easier for me to access their files by their first names. This is simply a preference.

Any related documents (e.g., court correspondence, family letters, school letters) are also included in the relevant client's section. All relevant documents are placed into the client's section. A section may contain forms for multiple clients. For instance, if I go to section *S*, I may have to sift through several stacks of forms to find the client I am looking for, even if it is alphabetically detailed. Therefore, I use large paper clips to fasten all of a client's documents. That way, as I flip through a section, I am not flipping through each individual document to find a person who may be in the back of the section: each client's section requires just one flip. I don't use staples. In the event that I need to remove a document, I want quick retrieval.

The client binders are kept in a portable briefcase that doubles as my laptop and tablet bag. The briefcase stays with me at all times. At the end of each day, I take it home, and each morning it comes with me to the office. This is for confidentiality protection. If I leave the files in my office and it gets robbed at night, those files of private information would be compromised. If I left them in my home office, it could get robbed when I am at my office, also compromising the files. Of course, this system is not perfect. When I was in a motorcycle accident in 2013, my portable case was on my bike, as the bike was my regular commuting transportation. When I awoke from my coma ten days later, I discovered that my files were no longer there. To this day, I have no idea what happened to them. My bike was wrecked, and pieces and parts were strewn across the street. My laptop and other belongings were destroyed. Even my clothing was cut off as paramedics tried to revive me. I don't know if the files were part of the loose wreckage that was cleaned off the street, if they blew away in the wind, or if they were accidentally put into the trash as crews cleaned the scene. Police and paramedics had no knowledge of the files, which is understandable: they were more focused on saving my life than they were on worrying about some random files that probably did not seem important. No plan is fail-safe.

Session notes are cumbersome and require quick and convenient access, so it is counterproductive to file them. I keep a small two-shelf cubby on my desk, and session notes are placed there for easy retrieval when a client arrives. The top of my handwritten notes are labeled with a client's initials so I do not confuse them. By the time a sheet is full, many of the notes are irrelevant, as the issues have been addressed. Relevant topics are transferred to a new sheet so new topics can be added. My retention is above fair, making it unnecessary for me to keep months and months of session notes to stay on topics. My session notes are typically bullet points that remind me of the details of our current conversations and strategies I've assigned to a client. I have found that if I neglect to take basic notes, I can be neglectful of current conversation topics, which compromises a client's confidence in me. We want to give an earnest impression to all clients that they and their issues are priorities to us, regardless of how busy we may be, how many other people we see, or how many private stressors we have.

Appointment Schedule

I'm a bit lazy with scheduling as well. For the first eight years, I used a week-at-a-glance scheduler. This tool has each week broken down by day and each day segmented by hours. At the end of the session, I would place a big X next to the appointment entry if the client paid and an O if he or she did not pay. At the end of each week, I would update invoices. Eventually I switched to my tablet for scheduling but continued to use the same notations. I initially began with a paper scheduler because I was concerned about data lost due to computer errors. And such errors happened—many times. Once to twice a year, my schedules are erased, disappear, or get somehow compromised, causing me to scramble to recreate them. The first time it happened, I resolved to keep both—an electronic schedule and written for backup—but I have not. My tablet now syncs with my smartphone and my laptop and even to my "cloud" service. With one entry, my appointment schedule exists in four places. I like this system. I like technology (when it works) and stubbornly refuse to go back to the paper schedule. So far, so good (lately). While any type of ledger you keep will permit you to add a quick note, tablets and smartphones have massive memory, and it is easy to enter and sustain most needed information, such as names and contact information. If I have a client named Bill, I enter his first name and last initial (Bill W.). If I have Bill's family members' contact information, I list them as separate contacts, such as "Bill W. Mom Katy." This system allows me quick access without having to search my memory. I know her as Bill W.'s mom, so she is entered that way. This system preserves some privacy and is effective, too.

Invoices and other account information are generated on my laptop and e-mailed, unless a client requests hard copies through the mail. I'm lazy here, too: only approximately 30 percent of my clients require any invoicing, so I only generate invoices for those who request them or run a balance. Billing documents are kept in a file on my laptop and are only printed and put into a client's file if needed. There have been a few times I wished I would've printed and filed a client's billing information, but only a few over eleven years, so I prefer my laziness here. Did I mention how much I do not like clerical work? Yeah, I really don't like it. I didn't become a counselor to do clerical work, and I prefer using my somewhat crude, lazy system to hiring someone. The expense and the burden of managing and routinely communicating with an administrative person are not justified for me. But if anyone wants to volunteer for this work, I'm open to it!

Court Referrals

Many clients are instructed by the court to be in a drug-treatment program and will require proof of attendance and participation to provide to a court, judge, or probation or parole officer. Some court agencies will require progress reports. Most courts have a list of preapproved programs, but typically any program that meets or exceeds similar criteria will satisfy the requirement. The following section includes samples of and templates for correspondence that can be used to satisfy court officials. These are actual letters I've used to assist clients, many of whom I've kept out of jail, giving them the opportunity to work, recover, and move on. Explanations of the documents are provided so you can gain knowledge of how to adapt and modify these to your own needs.

Student Exercises

- Make a list of requirements in your county to establish a DBA
- Ask your local bank how to establish a business account.
- Look into legal protection service.

NOTES

December 12, 2013

Attn: Criminal Judge

Re: Alexia S.

My name is Scott Spackey, and I am the principal owner and head counselor at Lifemind Alcohol & Addiction Treatment Counseling Center. I am also Alexia's individual counselor.

Alexia has been attending her sessions regularly and participating at a high level. Her progress here requires submitting to routine drug screens, engaging in weekly talk counseling, and completing homework assignments to become more self-reliant and independent for the future, as well as work on family relationships.

If anyone in the court should have any questions regarding her work with me, I am available almost anytime by phone and also by appointment. Please do not hesitate to contact me.

Scott Spackey, RAS, CHt, CLC

CATC #S0803130923

(PREVIOUS PAGE)

Alexia was facing possession charges that would result in fines and possible jail time. Her lawyer thought it would be best to preenroll in a program to show the court she was committed to improving and staying out of trouble. Providing proof she had enrolled into a drug-prevention and counseling program gave her defense attorney bargaining leverage, lessening her sentence to probation. Her sentence for possession became one year of probation and continued involvement in her counseling program with drug screens and monthly progress reports to her probation officer. Failure to comply with the program would be a violation of her probation and would mean six months in jail. She complied, I provided progress reports, and the family was grateful.

March 11, 2014

Attn: Probation Officer Henry T

Re: Tony K

My name is Scott Spackey, and I am the principal owner and head counselor at Lifemind Alcohol & Addiction Treatment Counseling Center. I am also Tony's individual counselor.

Tony completed a program that thoroughly covered the risks of alcohol and drug abuse on not only the self but the whole family. He was required to remain clean and sober for the duration of the program.

He participated at a high level and completed all tasks assigned to him.

If anyone in the court should have any questions regarding his work with me, I am available almost anytime by phone and also by appointment. Please do not hesitate to contact me.

Scott Spackey, RAS, CHt, CLC

California State License RAS #S0803130923

(PREVIOUS PAGE)

Tony was required to participate in a drug-treatment program as part of the terms of his probation. The letter confirmed and validated his attendance, and the court was satisfied.

CERTIFICATE OF COMPLETION

January 15, 2014

JAMES K. has completed Lifemind's drug/alcohol aversion and education program by participating in the following:

- private sessions
- group sessions
- goal- and strategy-setting activities
- personal risk evaluation

At this time I, Scott Spackey, Lifemind's head counselor and James's personal coach and instructor, hereby delegate James to a risk category of one regarding addiction and drug abuse, with one being the lowest risk and five being the highest. James would be well advised to consider involvement in social clubs or networks that promote clean living so he can become an accessible example of what it is like to live a fun and purposeful life without the use of intoxicants.

Scott Spackey, CHt, CLC, RAS

(PREVIOUS PAGE)

James had been suspended from his technical college because someone accused him of being involved with drugs. He insisted the allegation was not true, but the enrollment contract stated the college could expel him without tuition reimbursement for this offense, and they were not required to have proof or evidence. Before they would reinstate him as a student, the school demanded proof of attendance in a counseling program and results from drug screenings.

January 6, 2013

INVOICE

Alexia S.

C/O Bill S.

4339 Easy Street,
Santa Clarita, CA 91321.

Scott Spackey, State-Certified and Registered Addiction Specialist Counselor

RAS #S0803130923, TIN #93-1221306

Invoicing Billing Table for: Alexia S.

Recommended Diagnosis: 300.00 Recommended CPT:96152

Procedure/Treatment: H0007 (crisis intervention), H00047 (Other; management, prevention skills)

Type:	Date:	Services	Totals:	Status
1 Individual:	Nov 9, 2013	**H0001**	$135	**PAID**
1 Individual:	Nov 16, 2013	**H0001**	$135	**PAID**
1 Individual:	Nov 23, 2013	**H0001**	$135	**PAID**
1 Individual:	Nov 30, 2013	**H0001**	$135	**DUE**
1 Individual:	Dec 2, 2013	**Drug Screen**	$17	**DUE**
TOTALS:			$827	**PAID**

Balance Due: $152.00

(PREVIOUS PAGE)

This template is for invoicing. This type of statement is generated when a family needs to submit a claim to its insurance company for reimbursement.

RAS is my drug counselor registration number, which provides proof that I am a legally certified counselor. The TIN is a tax identification number. While many insurance companies require such a number, most do not. TIN is the number assigned to a business by the IRS for tax purposes. Although I have one, I am not required to because I am a sole proprietor with zero employees. My social security number is sufficient for the IRS, but it may not be accepted by some insurance companies.

"Diagnosis: 300.00" refers to the *DSM-V* code designating "anxiety state—unspecified."

I am always careful to provide diagnosis codes that indicate only temporary, or episodic, behavior, so as not to risk this code remaining on a client's record. While HIPAA assures that all documentation is confidential, we have to assume that someone, somewhere, can gain access to records. If this individual decided to pursue a career in law enforcement or federal government work, it is likely those codes and records could be accessed. If the codes designated a potentially permanent condition, like a chronic anxiety disorder, the individual could be disqualified from employment. Instead, the code indicates a temporary episode. Most *DSM-V* codes have both types of qualifiers: chronic and episodic.

CPT stands for "current procedural terminology"—the codes used in the insurance industry to justify claims and pay for treatment. These codes are copyrighted, and it is illegal for anyone but a licensed doctor to use them. This is why my statement says "recommended" before the CPT code. I cannot apply or use a CPT without violating the copyright. The invoice is stating that if she was to qualify for a CPT, I would recommend the one listed. Most insurance administrators need a code to fill in on their computer form in order to proceed to the next screen; if one is not entered, the process comes to a halt. Most insurance administrators are satisfied with the code and enter it. Only three times in twelve years has an insurance administrator refused the code because of the "recommended" qualifier.

HCPS stands for "health-care common procedure coding system." Similar to the CPT, these codes are used in the insurance industry for billing procedures. Without the code, a claim cannot be paid. The CPT codes are far more prevalent, as most insurance companies will not accept HCPS codes for billing, requiring the CPT codes instead.

In this instance, the family was determined to get reimbursement for the expenses of their daughter's treatment. They were not willing to go to an insurance-approved program because they found the approved programs to be too basic to be helpful. This is, unfortunately, a common sentiment.

This young client had involvement with heroin, which is what brought her to me. Her mother did not want a paper trail documenting her involvement with heroin. She adjusted the statement to include her anxiety and omitted the heroin issue. Her anxiety was very real: her life was in shambles as she desperately tried to recover from heroin addiction and to separate from most of her known associates, many of whom were addicts as well. Her drug abuse had severely affected her reputation at school and in her community. Who wouldn't have anxiety in such circumstances? Therefore, anxiety was a justifiable issue.

I have already recommended having the *DSM-V* in your personal library; it will also provide you with diagnosis codes (though you cannot diagnose, it is good to have access if needed). CPT and HCPS codes are available online for anyone to use.

In some instances, I have refused to place these codes on any paperwork whatsoever, unwilling to take the risk of using them. In those instances, I may mention verbally what I considered the correct code to be, along with a disclaimer: "I cannot provide you with codes without violating copyright laws or malpractice rules, as I am not a licensed doctor or an insurance-providing professional. All I can provide you with is an opinion of which codes I think one would use.

December 15, 2014

Re: Brandon P.

Dear Mr. Pillar:

My name is Scott Spackey, and I am the principal owner and head counselor at Lifemind Alcohol & Addiction Treatment Counseling Center. I am also Brandon's individual counselor.

Brandon began a counseling program with me on Saturday, November 22, 2014. He has participated in several sessions, and his family is involved as well. At this time, we are intensely working on several issues, including drug use and abuse, and assisting him to mature and become self-reliant and independent in a responsible way.

Brandon has agreed to submit to drug screening, and I am permitted to discuss the results of these tests with his family members if needed. Brandon has tested clean on his tests thus far. In addition, he participates in his individual and family sessions at a high level and completes all of the homework exercises I give to him. The family is committed to improving family dynamics for the entire household.

If anyone in the court should have any questions regarding his work with me, I am available almost anytime by phone and also by appointment. Please do not hesitate to contact me.

Scott Spackey, RAS, CHt, CLC

California State License RAS #S0803130923

December 30, 2014
Re: Brandon P.

Dear Mr. Chase:
I do not recommend a residential recovery program for Brandon at this time. The presence of his family and home are vital elements in his recovery, and I do not think he is a good candidate for the complicated environment of a recovery facility. The social dynamics can be overwhelming for many people and often be counterproductive, leading to relapses as a result of associating and cohabitating with other drug users and some criminal elements as well.

The outpatient program I have in place for him is as follows:

- one-on-one counseling sessions, three times per week
- family sessions once per week
- group meetings once per week (twelve-step program or other program)
- routine and frequent drug screening
- contact with a counselor each day
- work on recovery strategies and assignments, which include the following:
  - cognitive work (exploration of family issues and cause and prevention of drug abuse)

> ■ employment training (how to perform well in job interviews, conduct a job search, and select a career path)

(page 1 of 2)

(continued)

All of these program facets will be monitored and verified by the counseling team. Proof of completion of cognitive exercises is required.

At this time, Brandon is recommended to participate in this program for a minimum of ninety days. Once he has completed ninety days, an evaluation will be made to determine whether to continue with the same schedule or to lessen it. Regardless, he will continue in a program for an additional ninety days, or a total of six months.

At this time, the family does not have the resources to admit Brandon to a privately run facility, and the facilities available to him with no income would not be able to provide the most attentive treatment. LifeMind is cooperating with the family to provide affordable treatment that is customized for his personality and his issues.

Any program specifics and recommendations or court requirements will be applied. Feel free to contact me anytime to communicate additional criteria.

Scott Spackey, CHt, CLC, RAS

California State License RAS #S0803130923

These last two correspondences were for a young client awaiting criminal trial for robbery. He was accused of using an unloaded rifle to hold-up a pharmacy for benzodiazapenes. Working with his lawyer, we decided to offer the court a guilty plea in exchange for a light sentence of probation which participation of routine drug-screening and counseling would be mandatory and progress reports and updates would be provided to the court at each follow up hearing. Initially, this judge was open to an inpatient, residential program in lieu of jail time. I was certain that the young man would not be able to meet the strict, unforgiving, zero-tolerance policies of the facility and if he was ejected from their program he would go to prison. I had a very strong rapport with Brandon and felt confident he would do better out-patient and living at home. The judge agreed with one stipulation: That all tests must be verified and his attendance in counseling must be perfect. Brandon met the conditions and is now drug free, out of jail and working. It's been eighteen months since his criminal episode and drug use. He is grateful for being saved from jail and I am quick to remind him that if he does not comply with the tests and program as promised to the court that he will be in jail again. So far, so good.

8

WORKING WITH MINORS

(and Young Adults)

Working with minors is critical to your practice. From a counseling perspective, working with kids is both challenging and fulfilling. From a business perspective, parents are a lucrative market: they will spare little expense to help their kids, regardless of the child's age. If you can demonstrate progress and offer smart, insightful counseling, parents will provide the bulk of your income. I would estimate that 60 percent of my clients and income are related to those under twenty five. If you get results and a family likes you, you become something of a surrogate family member. I've had the honor of helping entire families, including different members of successive generations. A teen (always trouble!) is brought to you by a family who has difficulties or concerns regarding the teen. It is necessary to communicate with other family members over time to solve relevant issues or gain insights to family dynamics. Once the teen's issues are resolved, new ones appear—they're teens! Along the way, you become a trusted and respected advisor, and eventually a sibling or parent has an issue that needs attention. When this happens, you are the first person the family reaches out to. This is once again where versatility will pay off, for your clients and your practice. I met one family about their seventeen-year-old son, who had some social anxieties and was uncooperative with the family. I provided counseling to him for three years. During that time, his younger brother also had some issues, and the family asked me to counsel him. Over the five years I've known them, the mother and father have had separate sessions on parenting topics, and each parent has also used my services to reach personal goals and resolve personal issues. If I never retire, I may see their grandkids someday, too! This is a healthy, well-adjusted family who sees the benefit of assistance. They have a weekly cleaning service for the house, they take their car to a mechanic when it needs an oil change, and they visit a counselor (me) to help add clarity to their dynamics at home so they can focus on work, career, quality time, bonding, and things that truly matter. I'm honored as a counselor and appreciative as a businessman.

This section will cover the variety of counseling styles and attitudes and the unique ethical considerations and legalities that pertain to the demographic of minors.

Attitude

You are not under eighteen. Therefore youth automatically categorizes you, to some degree, as irrelevant and out of touch, regardless of your actual age. Young people have a built-in default brain wave that causes them to suspect all those they categorize as adults as conspiratorial. Most people under twenty-five categorize anyone over thirty and anyone who is a legitimate parent, homeowner and career-minded person as an adult.

Youths have powerful instincts. Because they have not yet been tainted by the commercial, practical need for results and productivity in society, they retain a semiblissful state of ignorance, which manifests as innocence. Youths have innocence, and this is wonderful and inspiring—and also maddeningly frustrating.

This innocence allows them to perceive people honestly. They can truly sense inauthenticity. Anyone they perceive as inauthentic is held at a distance, especially adults. They will instinctually refrain from being open or trusting with someone they perceive as inauthentic. They may not even know what the hell *inauthentic* means, but they do it!

In other words, if you *try* to be young, modern, hip, chill—*whatever*—it will work against you. Authenticity is much more valuable with them. Regardless of how out of touch you may be on current trends, fashion, or colloquialisms, you need to be yourself—that is, *authentic*. A seventeen-year-old will not resent you because you don't know who the current celebrities are or why they're in the tabloids this week. If you can acknowledge your ignorance—or even lightly joke about it—the youth will be happy to fill in the blanks for you and help you upload anything you don't know.

This will make them feel knowledgeable and respected; they know some things you don't and feel acknowledged when you defer to them on the right topics. If you demonstrate trust and a willingness to defer to them when they are the authority on a topic, they will subconsciously feel the impulse to defer to you when you are the authority on a subject.

Just as the adult world places significant emphasis on "just being yourself" to youth, this advice applies to adults as well: Be yourself, authentic and sincere. You will not only build needed rapport, but you will also set the example of authenticity, regardless of how embarrassing or different we can feel.

In the "Appearance" section, details are given on how to construct a look that is personal, authentic, current, and smart. Do not underestimate your appearance and your office environment as a marketing tool. People *do* judge books by their covers, and rightly so to some degree. If your appearance is slovenly, inappropriate, or counter to the impression you're trying to create, then it is proper to judge that cover! Remember that your appearance is an expression of who you are. Do not try to "youthenize" your appearance for your younger clients. Stick with your authentic self. While first impressions are not literally everything, they can set the tone for someone's perception of us.

It is commonly accepted that first impressions are everything, but this is not so. If a plumber comes to my home and is late, unapologetic, and somewhat rude, I will have a bad impression of him. However, if he does a phenomenal job, goes the extra mile, gives me a discounted rate for being late, and cleans up after the job like he was never even there, I am left with a great impression. Counterintuitively, I actually end up with a better impression than I would have had if everything had been perfect from the start. Due to the contrast, my final impression has greater emphasis. It almost makes good business sense to make a bad first impression. The contrast makes the good impressions really stand out!

Effective counseling requires you to make a good first impression, to be be steady throughout, and close with a powerful impression at the end of each session.

The Kids Are All Right

Young people rarely feel they are doing anything wrong with their lives and choices. The culture they belong to not only approves, but encourages their lifestyle. They are not evil or wrong or dumb or shallow (well...some of them). They are simply young and thus immature.

In their culture, cannabis, underage drinking, gratuitous sex, gossip, self-absorption, and self-entitlement are normal and common. Having been a resident of North America for my whole life, I feel that eating fish heads and pig entrails is gross and weird. But people in Asia and South America think *I'm* weird for wasting perfectly good food! They're not right, nor am I. They're not wrong, nor am I. We just have a cultural difference, same as adults and youth.

It is essential to avoid being judgmental. As an objective personality, your personal opinions are secondary. Providing information that is accurate, researched, well formed, and well articulated is primary. You can add your personal opinions to any subject, but be sure to categorize them as such: "In addition to that info, I personally feel that what you're involved in is a bad choice because..." and fill in the blanks. If you do not justify or explain your opinion in a way that is understood, then it is useless background noise. "Because I said so!" is a phrase we all made a promise not to repeat when we became adults one day.

It is important to lead a youth to conclusions and not tell him or her which conclusions to have. Treat them like adults, even if they are far from being or behaving like one. They will subconsciously sense this adult treatment and have an impulse to fulfill it. You would not tell adult clients how to be or how to act; you may suggest or recommend, but you would not tell them what to do. Youth expects adults to tell them to do things and are preprogrammed to resent and resist being told. By discussing, recommending, and suggesting ideas, you apply counterintuitive counseling rather than strong-arm tactics. It is not a guarantee they will perform or respond, but you can be assured they will defy and resist if you do strong-arm.

Youth lack the maturity to have powerful intuition of ethical connotations. They barely consider what their actions mean or how they affect others. When they do, their considerations are remote and brief. This is natural, not a defect: it is a symptom of youthfulness. Guide them, don't force.

Language

Become familiar with the common colloquialisms of current youth. Do not use them until you are familiar and comfortable with them. If you use them in the wrong place or in the wrong contexts, you will be perceived as forcing approval, and youths are typically repelled by this. Every generation has its own language. Typically, current terms and slang have several uses. SoCal in the 1980s saw words such as *rad* and *bitchen*, and *bad* has meant "good" for decades. Pay attention to your clients and to pop culture, and you will pick up current colloquialisms and how and when they're used. Over time, you will become familiar with them. Do not be embarrassed to ask what a term means. A confident person can acknowledge when he or she does not know something—only an insecure person would be ashamed to admit this. Once again, it's part of a healthy rapport to defer to the youth when appropriate.

Feel free to peruse slang dictionaries on the web. Slang terms stay relevant for quite some time. New ones are added pretty frequently, but existing ones do not disappear quickly. This book does not provide a reference list of current terms because I hope it will outlive the ones in fashion when it was written!

You need access to the most prolifically used colloquialisms, and it is all right to be slightly outdated if you are over twenty-five. If you actually speak in modern slang terms then you are, and will be perceived as, uneducated and immature. Slang terms are synonyms for actual terms and words, and you should have access to both. *Cool* has been around for sixty to seventy years and doesn't seem to be going anywhere. However, you should be able to express that feeling in legitimate, nonslang ways. When discussion is informal, slang is appropriate. When conversation is more formal, you need to be in the adult role—not the cool adult role, but the adult role.

Show your young clients how to shift gears and use proper terms in a dialogue. We wouldn't use slang in an interview for school or a job, so demonstrate the use of a variety in language so they learn from example.

Student Exercise
• Review current slang terms, pop-culture gossip topics (celebrities in the news), music trends and labels (e.g., techno, house, dubstep).

Chill

It is important to have a casual, informal dynamic with younger clients. Your lessons, coaching, and counseling need to be subtle. The messages and insights you want them to learn from you need to be woven into conversation. You will need to look for openings and opportunities to weave them in.

Every experience in life is an opportunity to learn and grow from. If a thirteen-year-old girl is complaining to about her bitchy BFF (best friend forever), this is raw material for life lessons. By exploring the issue of how the BFF was unfair and how wrong it was, your young client is validated. By expanding on the concept of how the BFF is an imperfect human (as we all are), the counselor can subtly teach about humility. Regardless of how the teen handled the BFF, the counselor can give a similar response. If the teen was rude to the BFF in an attempt to stand up for herself, the counselor can say something like the following: "Your reaction certainly seems justified. Anyone would be offended and upset. The only downside is that even though your reaction is normal, most people miss the point. If we use rudeness and anger in response to rudeness and anger, the point gets buried in the expression. But if you are calm and rational as you point out that you're hurt or offended by someone's lack of support, it almost shames the other person, showing by example, that his or her behavior was wrong. If you fight fire with fire, you just get more fire. I would encourage you to take the high road. It makes a stronger point."

If the teen took the BFF's abuse silently and is embarrassed by his or her passivity, an appropriate response would be something like the following: "It's normal to feel humiliated. That is why your friend treated you that way—to embarrass you. Don't give her the satisfaction. If you would've replied with sincerity to her, 'Ya know, that kinda hurt, and I feel embarrassed. I'm sure you didn't mean to, but...' your BFF would be embarrassed. See? You can turn the tables while maintaining your dignity. And you'd be far more mature than she was. That'd show her! The best revenge is living well! You tried to take the high road, and that is very mature. I'm proud of you. You should always stand up for yourself, but don't give anyone the satisfaction of making

105

you become the lesser, immature person. Not only will you feel better, but your friend might learn from you!"

Without using the term *forgiveness*, we've implied that forgiving is virtuous and that doing anything less is equal to the BFF's poor behaviors. The teen is now validated; you've bonded over the situation and dispensed advice in a noncritical manner, so it is received.

The client will subconsciously connect the dots and may inadvertently experience a small amount of guilt about mishandling similar conflicts with family members. However, it takes dozens—possibly hundreds—of these messages before action occurs. As a counselor, you cannot force clients to make use of the messages and insights you give them or dictate when to do so. Your duty and responsibility is to plant these seeds of knowledge and encourage them to grow.

Every story, anecdote, or drama in a youth's life is raw material that can be used to draw conclusions and make points in subtle and strategic ways. My son and I have bonded over baseball since he began to play at four years old. He has played and watched baseball throughout his life. Sports provide powerful metaphors for life, and any concept my son was not quite mature enough to process or understand could be explained in baseball metaphors and examples. I used baseball metaphors to explain the need for discipline in school, to navigate through girlfriend issues, and to demonstrate the importance of being on time, keeping one's word, being honest, following rules and laws—absolutely anything he needed to know. You can use sports, toys, TV shows, and pets. Everything and anything can be used as metaphor material, so long as it is something both you and the client are familiar with.

Minors Need Major Redundancy

Redundancy.

Did I say that already? Well, some things bear repeating.

I have made a joke to all of my clients about my penchant for redundancy and periphrasis. I offer my redundancy as a humorous fault of character and personality. I joke about this characteristic being compulsive so that clients will indulge me, but the truth is, I am fully aware of my redundancy (well, mostly anyway). I do it intentionally. People need to be saturated with an idea. Most people do not apply anything until it becomes so familiar that it is nearly tiresome. It's sort of like bunting a baseball: it is awkward because it is so different from actually hitting the ball. But as awkward as it is, once we level that bat to the ball over a dozen times, bunting becomes so familiar to us that it becomes second nature. Practice makes perfect.

See—I just slipped in the redundancy and a baseball metaphor to prove my point. The people who pick up on the redundancy and the metaphor may become ever so slightly annoyed, but not enough to find it offensive or call it out. Those who don't pick up on it receive the message anyway because it is subtly planted like a seed. Those who do pick up on it are fractionally inconvenienced by it, but it is still planted with them, too!

Redundancy is necessary with most clients, especially minors, but it must be well crafted. We cannot literally say the same thing the same way over and over again. We must find variations to express the same concept or lesson. Your redundancy must be subtly disguised, not too, too obvious. (Did I just say *too* twice?)

Sex

Sex is an important issue in everyone's life, and it is in the forefront of a youth's consciousness. You must be able to discuss it and yet be very cautious about it. You can and should allow youths to open up about their concerns, curiosities, and sexual activity. This sensitive area should only be discussed in objective terms, never personal or subjective. Do not share anything personal in this area. Only discuss sex in general terms with youth.

If a client (no matter how old he or she is) seems to be attempting to goad you into a sexual conversation, you must redirect it to *general* terms and concepts. Eventually, clients will get bored when you do not take the bait or even acknowledge their goading. If it is not entertaining to them, they will move on and likely never try goading you toward it again. If a client asks about your sexual preferences or tendencies, it is important to set a boundary that does not threaten rapport: "I try to have a very healthy sexual attitude—one that is not complicated and doesn't cause drama. Intimacy is important to us all, and I try to honor that. It's appropriate and important for us to discuss sexual issues, but unfortunately it needs to be a one-way street, as it isn't appropriate or productive for me to share. I want to be able to advise and support you. I don't blame you if you think it's unfair that you share and I don't and choose not to be open with me as a result, but I hope you can respect this guideline."

Adopt the role of a surrogate parent: sex talk between a child and his or her parent is awkward; a parent is rarely open to having frank discussions about sex. Give basics and acknowledge truths, but discourage in-depth, detailed discussions by subtly changing the direction. These topics should primarily be covered by parents, family members, or peers. Yes, yes—I know: a teen's peers are going to get it all wrong, and you may be trying to prevent incorrect and potentially toxic sexual ideation. This is why you need to be willing and able to have comfortable discussions about sex and subtly set the boundaries of those discussions. Take charge of the dynamic: it's your room!

Legal Intervention

You are required by law to intervene on a youth's behalf if that minor is a danger to himself or herself or others and also if he or she is at risk of physical or sexual harm. If a minor confesses to you that he or she is being beaten or sexually molested, it is your duty, obligation, and legal requirement to call the authorities and report it.

However, you must be careful. There are youths who know of this requirement and will put you in that position, even if it is not true. Sexual allegations could be a form of passive-aggressive punishment toward a parent or a misguided attempt to exercise control. You need to determine the authenticity of the implication or allegation.

When a sexual allegation has been inferred from a client who is a minor, you can interrupt and explain in gentle and reassuring terms, "I'm concerned. What you're describing sounds very upsetting, and I'm worried. I'm glad that you trust me enough to open up about this, and I want to respect that trust. As an adult I can't help but feel an impulse to intervene for you and try to protect you. It's important you understand that I am actually obligated to do something. If what you're implying is true, I may be required to intervene. Once a call is made to a protective agency, there is no taking it back. If what you're saying, or implying, is true, something needs to be done. It's normal for you to be scared of that, but we all must do what is honest and truthful in life, regardless of the consequences. But if what you've shared is incorrect, untrue, or an exaggeration, there is no taking it back. I'll tell you what: I'm going to process what you've told me and take a little time to consider it, and before I do anything, we're going to talk about it again. OK?" This reaction is only acceptable if there is not an immediate threat, risk, or danger. If danger is immediate, intervention is urgent: in such a case, it is an ethical and legal requirement to intervene immediately.

Every community has a local government agency that is responsible for protecting children. This is the agency you would contact. Once contacted, the agency will open a case, assign an agent to it, and begin a procedure. The procedure begins with a visit to the home, which is typically unannounced. Agents will interview the parents and the child and assess the situation. Once this begins, there is no way to stop it. The parents may lose custody: the child could be remanded into foster care or a facility for protection. If someone is truly in danger, this is necessary. If an individual is not in danger, however, the trouble that will ensue can ruin lives and families. Child Protective Services is a bureaucracy. It follows protocol and procedures and does not adapt or customize itself well to situations that are not textbook. The majority of agents working for the agency are underpaid, undereducated, and underqualified. They know how to follow procedures—and they do—but not much else. I have witnessed appropriate interventions that have saved lives, but I have also seen many instances in which kids were returned to dangerous parents because the parents fulfilled the criteria of counseling and education and were monitored over probationary periods, satisfying the courts. I've also watched decent, harmless parents lose children to the protective system and go through years of torment before restoration occurred. This is a serious and grave decision that cannot ever be taken lightly. The wrong decision could not only end your career, but it could also destroy a family and a child. Child Protective Services makes mistakes. The agency is not infallible. And these mistakes can make the phrase "ruin lives" seem frivolous.

Kids: There Oughta Be a Law Against Them!

Working with minors will require you to be quick thinking and decisive, yet if you make impulsive decisions without thought and clarity, you can cause damage to them, to yourself, and most certainly to your career.

When I first started out, I swore I'd never work with kids. I found them annoying, and their lack of maturity and inability to carry a conversation were not features I thought I could tolerate. To me, they were dumb, selfish, narrow-minded and self-absorbed. I didn't work so hard to become an adult just to spend all my time with kids. I left junior high in the past—and high school, too—for good reason!

But all of that changed. Now I would rather spend my days in sessions with the youth. I love their innocence, their honesty, their willingness to try, and their openness

110

to ideas. Adults are the ones who think they know everything worth knowing and are consciously resistant to change and humility (ironic, huh?). Youth respond to authenticity, not to impressions. Most of them are eager for conversations that are not superficial; they are starved for mature, intellectual interaction. They're my favorite clients. Most adults are dull. Too many adults are narrow-minded and self-absorbed, and they, unlike the youth, should know better! Most youth are dynamic and seeking.

I like seeking.

9

HARM TO SELF OR OTHERS

Danger to Themselves

If someone is a danger to himself or herself or others, you are required to call the authorities—the police, the sheriff, Child Protective Services—an appropriate *government* authority or agency. Be very thorough and cautious. Once authorities are involved, it is nearly impossible to stop the wheels of bureaucracy from turning. While it is far better to err on the side of caution, making a mistake here can be life altering. The majority of people who threaten or voice an intention of suicide are not actually suicidal. The majority of those who actually commit suicide do not threaten, voice, or outwardly acknowledge their intention. Those who attempt suicide are usually calm and rational— not hysterically emotional. Even though many are not seriously suicidal, their pleas for help and intervention are.

"Sometimes I feel like killing myself" is something most everyone says at one time or another. "Sometimes I think it'd be easier if I just wasn't here anymore" is a normal and common musing from someone in crisis. Very few people act on this or are even truly considering it.[8] Many people who feel overwhelmed will express a wish to die, which is in fact a desire to be liberated from what is overwhelming them. By interviewing them, we can navigate through the concern to determine whether a serious intervention is needed. The following questions can be useful:

---

[8] There are approximately forty thousand suicides in the United States each year, of over three hundred million people (CDC.gov).

112

- How often do you think of this?
- That's sad and sounds tragic. Are these thoughts episodic and brief, or are they consistent? In other words, do you feel this way consistently or only when things are particularly tough, as they have been lately?
- What kind of a difference would that make?
- What do you suppose the purpose to life is? (This initiates a dialogue about bigger picture concepts)

Case Conference

I had been counseling a woman with borderline personality disorder for six months; we'll call her Cathy. One night she threatened suicide to her mother. The mother phoned me to intervene. I placed calls to her psychiatrist, but there was no reply. The doctor's answering service suggested I call 911. Calling the doctor was a dead end.

I spoke with Cathy on the phone to evaluate the situation. Her disorder frequently manifested as intense episodes of crisis. Her mother and other family members were emotionally held hostage during these episodes. If they left her alone or didn't give her complete attention, she threatened to kill herself. These episodes had been going on for years, and her family members were so frustrated that they were tempted to just abandon her when they occurred. Historically these episodes had been attempts to get attention. She had no history of suicide attempts—just threats.

As I spoke with Cathy, I sensed she was sincerely distressed but not seriously suicidal. I explained to her, "Everyone is very scared and nervous and does not want to make a mistake here. As I think you know, I am required—by law—to report this. Once I do, sheriffs will be dispatched. They will be required to take you into custody, and you will be placed on a seventy-two hour hold at the local behavioral-health unit. They will medicate and monitor you."

Her demeanor shifted. She was still distressed, but she was suddenly rational. If she had begun pleading with me not to call the sheriff, this would've indicated that she might have been serious about her threat. Had she become enraged or angry, that would've indicated a serious threat. Had she become calm and peaceful and made no attempt to discourage my contacting the authorities, this may have indicated an intense need for intervention and attention, and I would've called. If she had been admitted, by the time she was released (three days later), she would never make that threat again simply to get attention. The behavioral unit is not a pleasant place. It is a dorm for mentally unstable and emotionally compromised people. The food is horrible, the beds are uncomfortable, and the environment is disturbing and sometimes dangerous. A percentage of the patients there are angry and can be violent, intimidating, or both. Because I knew this woman had been to the behavioral-health unit before, I invoked its memory to motivate her getting some control over herself: "Please understand that if you attempt suicide, we will intervene, and you will awake from your sleeping-pill suicide attempt in the behavioral-health unit. That is where this will end up. You won't die, because family and I will intervene because we care for you. You will live, but you may suffer some sort of permanent damage to your brain or organs as a result, in addition to the trauma of the experience itself. Things could get much worse, or they could get better. It's up to you."

She changed her mind and rationally persuaded us that while she was not well, she was not *actually* suicidal. I agreed to not call authorities on the following conditions:

1. You will need to remain in sight to your family. You may not be left alone. If you leave and are unattended, sheriffs will be called, and they will find you and take you in.
2. You are required to make contact with me every two hours. You may call me directly or have your parents call. If I do not get that call, I will assume

something has happened, and I will fulfill my obligation to call the sheriff.

3. For the rest of the evening, you will try to rest and have some food and watch TV or entertain yourself frivolously: television, games, puzzles, drawing—anything that is simple and helps pass the time and appears normal so your parents can perceive you're all right.

"Do we have an agreement?" I asked.

She agreed, and we got through the night. Cathy's family was never again subjected to suicidal threats during her manic episodes. She continued to have manic-depressive episodes, but no threats of suicide were ever mentioned during them. I spoke with her psychiatrist the following day. I explained to him my credentials, and he was surprisingly respectful. I shared my nonclinical theory that she had many of the criteria for borderline personality disorder, and I asked what the doctor thought of that assessment. He said that it was an interesting perspective to consider and that he would give it more thought.

Many doctors will not treat patients with borderline personality disorder because they are difficult and can be very disruptive to one's practice and personal life. In fact, several days later, this doctor dropped Cathy as a patient. A private-practice counselor can expect to encounter many shortcomings of the system.

To this day I feel confident about my intervention. It restored peace, established safety, and forced Cathy to be more accountable for her disorder. She is not a bad person for having an episode and involving her family in it. She is a victim of a debilitating disorder and not entirely accountable. However, containing it within the family allowed her to avoid traumatic visits by the sheriff and trips to the hospital.

Initially, I regretted even mentioning the word *borderline* to her doctor. It was clear he had not previously drawn that conclusion, and once it was made obvious to him, he dropped her as a patient. Cathy was very angry with me at first. Ultimately, she came to the realization that her doctor was not a true ally and not committed to her as a patient or person. He hadn't even referred her to another doctor—he simply dropped her. This scenario brought out his true colors.

Last I saw her, Cathy had finally accepted that she was borderline and was committed to specific practices and strategies for improvement. I helped her to find an appropriate program in LA. There aren't very many. Borderline personality disorder is a disproportionately neglected disorder.

Dual Diagnosis, Co-Occurring Disorders

Many clients may qualify as dual diagnosis or co-occurring disorders by exhibiting more than one disorder such as ADD, bi-polar and addiction. It is imperative to try to refer these clients to a specialist you can regularly consult with. Do not simply refer them to a doctor, but to a doctor who specializes in the particular disorder. Try to build a relationship with other local professionals that will allow some consultation contact to serve mutual clients. Many professionals will appreciate your referral and willingness to defer your work with them,

Danger to Others

"My husband made me so mad the other night, I wanted to kill him!"

"My wife pissed me off so bad yesterday, I thought I was gonna kill her!"

"Sometimes my parents are so mean, unfair, and evil. I wish they were dead."

None of these comments necessarily warrant a call to 911. They are common expressions of anger and other emotions. A real threat involves a plan. By carefully interviewing a client, you can better discern whether a threat is sincere or not.

Does the client seem to have a plan? Are the client's statements symptoms of an obvious and intense emotional episode? If so, he or she will likely move on from the idea once he or she calms down, and there was never anything to truly worry about. However, if the client seems calm and rational during these threats, that is cause for alarm. Someone considering doing harm to another person in a calm, rational manner is a serious threat.

What's more disturbing? A raving, yelling person who is making threats or a calm, serene person with a blank look in his eyes who says with utmost calm, "I'm going to kill you"?

It's pretty normal to wish pain on people you feel deserve it for who they are or what they've done. It doesn't make us bad people if these thoughts come to mind. It is unfortunately natural to feel anger to a point of wanting harm to come to someone. While I may damn the person who cut me off in traffic and even think bad thoughts about him, the thoughts remain in my own head. I would never act on them; they are normal and will pass.

I hope I get to the point where I do not get angry over minor transgressions and can instantly forgive or not be bothered by them at all. Alas, I'm simply not that evolved! However, though I may wish a flat tire on someone, I sure wouldn't cause it! When I catch myself wishing for vengeance, I acknowledge that this is a common behavior; it's not a crime to think such things. I also acknowledge that I would be a better person and much happier if I didn't think them. I allow myself to feel a tiny bit of shame rather than excusing it. I don't rationalize my harmful thoughts. I accept that it is common to have them and commit to maturing beyond them. And I attempt to redirect them to anything irrelevant while it passes, minimizing my time spent with toxic thoughts and feelings.

If you get a clear sense a client may harm someone, authorities must be called. Try to bring some sense to the person, but follow through with the call. If you learn that a client has already harmed someone, authorities *must* be called. This is the law and is not a violation of counselor-client confidentiality. You're not an attorney; you're a counselor!

Spousal Abuse

Most domestic violence victims try to protect their abuser for two reasons: they don't want ensuing consequences, and their feelings are conflicted.

Consequences

Many victims of abuse are afraid of the additional abuse they will eventually receive once their abuser learns of their accusation. In most cases, this is a real threat. An abuser will often turn more violent if provoked by disclosure. Such individuals may go into a rage and try to "teach their partner a lesson" with more abuse. The results are devastating: hundreds of thousands of spouses are beaten, and some even killed, once the abuser discovers they alerted authorities. Most of the time, law enforcement is required to take accused abusers into custody with nothing more than an accusation. Once in custody, they wait for an arraignment, and if the abused victim does not testify, the abuser is released. Now violent and angry, the abuser may be bent on revenge, and the abuse victim is in real trouble.

Conflicted Feelings

Though an abuse victim can be justifiably angry and want to abandon the abusive partner, the two have a long and complicated history, and our minds define pleasure as that which is familiar. Abuse victims are familiar with these toxicities, and their subconscious creates uncertainty to protect the paradigm it knows, even though it is dangerous.

Case Conference

A forty-three-year-old woman came to see me about her husband's alcohol abuse. In her second session, I asked her what she thought about trying to invite her husband to a session to intervene on his drinking.

"No. He would never come. And he would get very angry."

"How would he react if you asked him?"

"He would get very angry and accuse me of trying to ruin his reputation."

"And...?" I sensed she was holding back.

"He can get rough. My husband is a decent man who cares for me, but when I make him very angry...well...I don't want to start with him."

"Does he get rough? Shove, push, hit, break things?"

Her answers were becoming more sheepish. "Yes. He could."

"I want you to know that I am not required by law to report anything you tell me and would never do so without your permission. You're an adult, so everything we talk about is confidential. But this sounds serious. Does he hurt you?"

"Oh, yes. He's bruised my face and body before. Many times. It's only when he's really mad, though."

It took a while to earn her trust, but after a couple of sessions, it was clear that she was in real danger and intervention was needed. She also had a young daughter at home. She assured me her husband was never violent with the daughter, but the nine-year-old girl was clearly

119

traumatized by witnessing the violence inflicted on her mother.

It took me six weeks to convince my client to protect herself. I did so by placing emphasis on her daughter: "Even if he never touches your daughter, she is being emotionally abused by seeing her mother beaten. This is traumatizing her. She may not have a chance at a healthy relationship with a man or ever consider having a family as a result. And it is likely that it is only a matter of time before your husband directs his violent lack of respect for women toward her. Men who are violent with women do not simply get better: they get progressively worse. Today it's black eyes; tomorrow it's a sprain or something broken. And in five years, it's trips to the hospital, until one of these episodes goes too far. Don't risk traumatizing your daughter. If you don't take some action for yourself, do it for her. She needs your protection. She needs someone who is rational and willing to do what is right for her. She is too young and inexperienced to manage this."

I had already determined to closely monitor the situation and was poised to intervene in their behalf by calling child-protection officials.

Over several weeks, I helped the client covertly develop a strategy to leave the home, and I facilitated her meeting with the local shelter for battered women, who assisted her with shelter and employment-training opportunities so she could one day support herself. Like many abused wives, her material dependence on her husband had been a major factor in remaining with him.

While living at the shelter, she often regretted her decision. Even eight months later, she wondered if she'd made the right decision. Life was uncomfortable and uncertain. Three years later she was living in an apartment and employed as an office assistant, and her daughter was going to school. The husband tried counseling and was forced by the court to attend counseling and parenting classes. By the time he was eligible to have child visitation, he had relocated to another community, virtually abandoning his wife and child.

She has a tough life, but knows she made the right call.

I've counseled many women through this, and the majority of them end up staying in the abusive relationship. It is hard to witness and hard not to intervene. It makes you consider giving up when you see people refuse your help and advice despite the suffering they are going through. It can make it hard to come to the office sometimes. But the few that make it through make it worthwhile. If I help just one out of a hundred, that's one less person who's suffering.

A counselor needs to be resilient. It is often suggested that we shouldn't emotionally care about those we help and that we shouldn't get involved. That goes against every reason I started this career. I *do* care. I care a lot, and it is very emotional when harm comes to my clients.

You can care as much as you want, but remember your role. You are a sensible mentor, not anyone's savior or superhero. You're there to help and assist in any way you can that is sensible and does not jeopardize your career. If you jeopardize your career, you will not be able to help anyone—not your current clients or those you've yet to meet. Don't forget that charity begins at home. Take care of *you*. Take care of your loved ones. Meet your responsibilities and commitments to them. Once you've done that, give everything you have left of yourself to those who've trusted you, as a professional, to help them.

10

ADDICTION COUNSELOR

Each state has different requirements one must meet in order to legally provide addiction-counseling services, but the basic requirements are similar:

- 150 (+/-) hours of formal education
- 160 (+/-) hours of supervised clinical experience (i.e., an internship)
- successful completion of state exam
- 2,100 (+/-) hours of clinical experience (providing counseling)

In addition to fulfilling these initial requirements, 40 (+/-) continuing-education units (CEUs) must be verified every two years for renewal. CEUs are available online at many sites, such as CE4Less.com.

Let's examine the requirements in more detail.

Formal Education

Qualified schools will have a curriculum of topics for you to study and be tested on. The material has been evaluated and estimated to take 150 hours of time to complete. This number fluctuates. A more adept student might be capable of completing the curriculum in 100 or even 50 hours. A less adept student may need more than 150 hours to complete the curriculum. The material is what needs to be completed, and it is valued at roughly 150 hours. Below is a list of the course titles from my certification program to give you an idea of the curriculum:
- Cultural Differences/Special Populations
- Prevention and Education

- Legal and Confidentiality Issues/Ethics /Prevention of Sexual Harassment
- Self-Help and Twelve-Step Therapy
- HIV/ARC/ AIDS/Communicable Diseases
- Role of the Counselor
- Individual Counseling Techniques
- Group Counseling Techniques
- Dual Diagnosis/*DSM-IV*/Co-occurring Disorders/PTSD
- Internship Process
- TAP 21 and Twelve Core Functions
- Case Management

Each subject required reading material from a textbook and then taking an exam. The tests were always multiple choice and contained between 75 and 150 questions. Some exams required a few essay answers, typically less than a page long.

It can be tempting to first read the exam questions and then skim the text to look for the answers. While this may get you ahead of schedule and a passing grade, I do not recommend it. You will not likely retain (or even learn) valuable information.

Supervised Clinical Experience

You must work in the field of addiction counseling as an assistant or trainee to gain practical experience while being supervised by a certified professional. For most interns, duties include filing, reception (answering phones), participating in counseling sessions, billing, and even getting coffee! The intern is there to help the facility run smoothly and is usually asked to address much of the tedium of running a program, thereby liberating the staff from these duties so they can focus on clients. I interned for the National Council on Alcoholism and Drug Dependence (NCADD). NCADD is a government-funded program for drug issues, and many drug offenders are remanded to it to satisfy the court. If these offenders do not complete the NCADD program, they face jail time. I typically went three times per week, and the staff (three counselors and one manager) allowed me to be very flexible in my schedule. My duties included filing, completing administrative paperwork (filling out forms for and about clients for the courts and for the NCADD records), sitting in on group and individual counseling sessions, and administering on-site drug tests to males, as I was one of the only males on site.

State Exam
Most schools will assist you in scheduling and registering for your state's exam. Exams are typically made up of 150 to 300 multiple-choice questions with several essay questions of 300 to 500 words (a few paragraphs or one page). The exam is typically timed, and you are given two to four hours to complete it. This varies depending on the state and the size of the exam.

Clinical Experience
Time spent working as a counselor is required[9]. Technically, you are not certified until you have completed the clinical hours, but while your certification is pending, you are legally allowed to function as a counselor. Once the clinical hours have been submitted and confirmed, your certification becomes full and active[10].

Every two years, roughly forty CEUs must be verified in order to renew a license. CEUs are available online at

---

[9] My clinical hours were performed at my own practice. I began counseling substance-issue clients privately and documenting the time devoted to those specific issues. I collaborated regularly with other, more experienced counselors to gain insight and receive assistance. My 2,100 hours were verified by the certified counselors I conferred with and a friend who was a part-time administrator and assistant volunteer for my practice.

[10] The training course that coincides with this book and *Project Addiction* is equal to 1,800 verified clinical hours. Go to www.ProjectAddictionCounselor.net for details or to register.

many sites, such as CE4Less.com. These online providers are legitimate and used for many service positions, including psychologists, Marriage Family Therapists (MFTs), school counselors, nurses, social workers, and others in the helping field. They typically offer multiple-choice exams corresponding to provided reading material. The forty hours is an approximate value based on the topics, subjects, and curriculum. Most people will complete this material with a total of ten to fifteen hours of actual work.

Why Do We Need Legal Certification?

To be a private-practice drug counselor, legal license is required. Many recovery facilities have staff members that are not licensed, and the ratio criteria varies from state to state. If you are not legally licensed or certified, you will likely not be compensated very much, if at all.

For example, currently in the state of California, 30 percent of a recovery center's counseling staff must be legally certified to provide counseling. That is only three out of ten staff members. Usually only those who are legally registered and certified receive compensation; the rest of the staff is typically unpaid or paid minimally. Recovery facilities take advantage of program alumni, often exploiting them to provide counseling to clients and families and offering zero or little compensation. In other words, addicts are not receiving trained help, and untrained help is being exploited for profit. If you want to be taken seriously and make a living as an addiction counselor, you will need to be licensed. If you want to make this a career and have a private practice, legal certification is required.

Check your state's requirements.[11] Typically, certification from another state is not automatically transferable; you must have certification that is recognized by the state you

[11] Visit www.humanservices.edu/substance-abuse-counselor.html# for state-by-state requirements.

are providing in. Most states allow you to transfer your educational units toward their licensing, only requiring you to take their state exam to provide counseling in their state. I am certified in the state of California. If I relocated to Oregon, I could provide counseling by providing proof of equal or greater academic education units and meeting their required amount of work experience. With this evidence, I would qualify for the state exam, which I would need to pass in order to be certified in Oregon.

At the time of this writing, I am not aware of any state in the United States that prevents a certified counselor from providing private-practice service. The laws do not require a special certification, license, or permit to provide services privately. Absolutely anyone can begin an addiction program or facility, but typically only certified counselors can provide the actual counseling.

When I began my legal certification process, I interviewed many schools, asking what the limitations were regarding where I was legally permitted to provide counseling.

"Can I run my own private-practice counseling center?" I asked at one school.

"Uh...I don't know. No one ever asked me that before," the individual responded. School administrators said they'd verify with the school's principal and other senior administrators and get back to me. Three days later they called and explained that there was nothing in the laws in California stating that one could run a private practice, but nor was there anything stating that one *couldn't*. "It just isn't done. No one here has ever heard of anyone doing that. It's not illegal...so..."

I already had an office for my life-coaching and hypnotherapy services. I already had a waiting room and business cards and a website. I knew that with small modifications I could market my practice to include addiction-counseling services.

So I did.

Many people are attracted to the privacy of a private practice. They do not want to attend meetings in their own community and risk making their substance issues common knowledge. They do not want a residential program that could threaten their jobs, education or family life by being away for too long. They need outpatient treatment, and they do not want a general practitioner of psychology or psychiatry. They want a specialist. Eighty percent of my clients with substance-abuse issues have been under twenty-five, and their families did not want them going to meetings or rehabs where they would be exposed to other drug users and addicts, which is a genuine and appropriate concern.

A common joke in the addict culture is, "If you can't find anywhere to score dope, you can always go to a meeting or to rehab!" Going to meetings, rehabs, or jail is a sure way to score dope since someone there is always holding!

These concerns are what will motivate people to call you, but it is service and results—their progress—that keep them coming and committing. It is results that built my reputation and results that made my practice lucrative.

"If you build it, they will come" is a famous line from the film *Field of Dreams.*

Addiction is so pervasive and common in modern culture that if you open a practice and can legally provide recovery service, "they will come." However, only the strong survive. As a solo practitioner, you will require results to keep your business alive and thriving. Anyone can open an office, but only good and effective counselors will be able to sustain one.

The established recovery industry has massive working capital for big advertising and accessibility (e.g., multiple locations and large, comfortable facilities). A large company with good salesmanship can easily withstand the loss of clients because of an already high client volume and expensive treatment. Interestingly, the established recovery industry (rehabs and residential facilities) has a success rate lower than 10 percent. Most recovery facilities conveniently avoid accountability, claiming, "If it didn't work, it must be the client's fault." While to some extent this is true, the logic of it is conveniently twisted: "If only ten percent of the driveways I poured stayed intact, I would be out of business in three months" said an addiction client who owned and operated a cement company.

I do not know of any business that can survive with less than 20 percent success, other than the medical and recovery industry. As a private-practice counselor, I knew I would be out of business in a short time with only 10 percent of my clients making progress or referring me, and rightfully so.

Addiction Education

The material covered in state-required addiction-treatment education is fundamental and basic. Much of it is essential information to be able to perform this duty; however, most veteran addicts and mature adults are reasonably intuitive, making the useful parts rather elementary.

In my training, there was an entire section, long and arduous, that detailed the percentages of different races and cultures and the statistics on their respective addictions (Cultural Differences/Special Populations). I did not see how I could help someone by informing him or her that people of Asian origins were 25 percent less likely to develop issues with alcohol than white or black Americans due to Asian flush syndrome. Unless my client was an Asian alcoholic, that information was useless trivia.

I never saw a moment in which I could dissuade any alcoholic from drinking—regardless of race—by knowing this factoid. But I needed to know it to pass the certification exam in California.

Many schools teach only the basic knowledge one needs to pass the exam, but there are also schools that offer extensive training. I have friends who attended two-year programs at community colleges or one-year programs at universities. I have no doubt that the quality of education they received was proportionate to the costs. Many programs are extensive and thorough and go well beyond state requirements, and such programs are recommended. However, your choice should be based on your experience and ability. These are discussed in detail below.

Experience

- Are you an addict?
- How long did you use?
- What was the extent of your drug use?
- How did you get clean?
- How long have you been clean?
- What have you accomplished in life*?
  *Other than sobriety, what conventional accomplishments do you have (e.g., a career, a family, or other successes) that people can relate to and also want for themselves?

Ability

- Can you articulate, express yourself, and communicate well?
- Can you adapt to different personalities?
- Can you relate to many different social cultures (e.g., single people, married people, family people, kids, religious people, agnostics, professionals, the unemployed, people of different nationalities, and so on)? (The aforementioned Cultural Differences/Special Populations class did not address the need to be somewhat cross-cultural at all!)

These categories are detailed and explained in *Project Addiction*, which also teaches readers how to deal with every addiction and habit. *Project Addiction* may be the only manual that separates every drug and behavior and provides specific treatments for each one, rather than addressing addiction in general. An addiction to meth is vastly different from an addiction to heroin. They both work on the same principles, but the two drugs are very different, and thus very different types of personalities are drawn to and become addicted to them. Addicts know this, but the recovery industry neglects this by conveniently lumping all addictions together as if they are the same. They're not. At all.

Adapting

You are the professional, and *you* will be required to adapt your personality and thinking to your client's, not the other way around. If you can only adapt to a small margin of society, you will not be able to sustain a full-time practice. The subject of versatility is explored in more detail in the section entitled "Life Coach," and is essential to understand.

The role of an addiction counselor is pivotal. You are given a great responsibility. The people employing you are vulnerable and confused. Many of them are at a crossroads in their lives. You cannot underestimate your role: if you mislead people or misadvise them, people can die. Overdoses, suicides, insanity, and permanent impairments can result from poor addiction counseling. If a facility fails and someone dies, the severity of the situation is somewhat remote. But if a private-practice counselor fails and someone's life goes badly south, there is great accountability. This is not just a job. It is a duty and responsibility that will account for a turning point in many people's lives. Which way that individual will turn is undecided, but he or she certainly will.

It is imperative to provide the best service you can. You must feel confident that if a client truly applies what you are advising, he or she will progress. If a client follows all of your strategies and does not progress, then it is clear those strategies are not correct for that particular client. It is unreasonable to believe you can save every client, but each treatment must be customized to each individual—his or her drug, personality, and dynamics (family, job, and so on). If treatment is not customized, it can't work. Every individual is different, and so is every drug and behavior, making it imperative to provide customized strategies. If a client fails it is the fault of both the client and the counselor. The only way a program, facility, or counselor is not accountable is if the counselor customized a program and the counselor and the client both agreed that it would work and was within the client's ability to execute, but the client did not do what was agreed upon.

I cannot count the number of clients who came to me after "failing" their fourth or fifth recovery program and were giving up. They had a quality about them; it was as if their soul or spirit had been drained. They were convinced they were worthless and hopeless because their families had spent thousands and rehab had housed them for three months, teaching everything it knew, and yet they had failed. "Relapse is part of recovery" is a colloquialism of recovery that seems to provide a self-fulfilling prophecy: addicts expect to relapse, and so they do. The addictive mind is searching for any rationale it can exploit. If an addict feels he or she is expected to relapse, the addict mind will use that. Relapse *is* often—in fact usually—a part of recovery. It often takes failures to reinforce the significance and needed magnitude of recovery commitment. But just because relapse is usually a part of recovery does not mean it has to be!

Addicts who relapse can too easily accept that they had only done what was their nature, yet they still absorb the weight of blame and shame for all those who believed in and hoped for them. It's a mixed message when a rehab client uses and is told to leave: essentially they're told that relapsing is part of recovery, but get out.

These treatment failures often become the final step in an addict's surrender, the final, most acute stage of addiction, during which addicts accept their pathology by making a subconscious, spiritual decision to live with their using because they cannot triumph over it. Many do not return from this stage: they live as using addicts for the remainder of their lives.

Many addicts reach out in desperation and are told to conform to a sobriety program. An inability to do so is seen as failure, and they begin to believe they are beyond redemption. Programs must adapt to them, not the other way around!

When a client progresses in recovery, the program gladly accepts partial credit for the success, yet when an addict uses or fails, a program rarely shares in the accountability.

Being Accessible

Being an addiction counselor is a demanding role. We are on call nearly 24-7. It is important for your clients and essential to your practice that you be accessible to your clients when they need you, not when it's convenient or during business hours. This does not mean you cannot have an existence outside of our practice. You need to take care of your personal needs and your family's needs as well. Personal and family needs are the priority above all else, but it is necessary for family members to be supportive of your role as a counselor.

When you are at dinner, on vacation, or at your daughter's soccer game or your son's acting performance at grade school, you should definitely pay attention and be present, both physically and mentally. But clients have a sixth sense: they always manage to call at the most awkward times. The phone rings when you're on the way out the door or as your son comes to bat at the game or just as your meal arrives at your romantic dinner. Below is some advice on how to handle such situations.

1. Look at your phone, see who it is, and go back to your dinner or child's game.
2. Advise your loved one, "In a few minutes, I need to go outside to make a call. Someone's in crisis."

It is natural for family members to be irritated and feel they are secondary. However, your practice is your source of revenue to pay for that dinner and sports gear, and your family needs to recognize that many people are not so fortunate and that their comfortable life is supported by those who are suffering and need help. Your family will need to have perspective.

You cannot abandon family plans every time a client calls, nor is it possible to answer at the moment the client calls. When you are aware that a client is reaching out to you for help, advise your family that sometime within the next twenty to thirty minutes, you need to excuse yourself to help someone and that it may take five to twenty minutes. Texting is wonderful in such situations. Text the client, "I'm tied up at the moment, but I will call in about twenty minutes. If it's absolutely critical and you're not safe, I will call now."

Ninety-nine percent of clients will appreciate your effort and apologize or excuse you altogether. One percent will say they're in crisis and need you to call immediately. The ones who excuse you from calling need to be called back as quickly as you can without total disruption to your family. The 1 percent in crisis need to be called immediately! Do not offer to call 911 or advise them to. They reached out to you for a reason, and if you're not OK with that, then you should never have assumed the role of mentor to begin with. Call them and assess whether a 911 call is needed. The clients who are not in crisis will often feel bad about contacting you. Here is a sample of a graceful reply:

"I'm glad you called. I would feel bad if there was something I could've kept from getting worse and you never reached out. I've only got a few minutes, but tell me what's going on."

Set their mind at ease, and transfer the topic from you to them and their issue. This reply subtly reminds the client that the timing is inconvenient, which sets timing parameters: the client already knows you will only be on the phone for a few minutes.

Listen to the client's issue. If he or she is rambling, you must control the conversation by interjecting, "You're truly upset and that is understandable. Back up a few steps, and tell me like I'm a two-year-old so I can follow along."

Once the client responds, say, "OK, good. Hold on a minute so I can reply to your problem and process it, too. I've already got some suggestions and want you to know them before we run out of time." Give a few one- to three-sentence suggestions and instructions. Be clear and direct. Then follow with a question: "Do you think you got that? Want me to repeat it? OK, good. Now, you mentioned another part...what was it?"

Address the next issue the same way, with one- to three-sentence instructions. Tell the client that he or she did the right thing by calling you: "I'm glad you called. Better to call now than to wait until our scheduled appointment. Things could've gotten worse. Try what I'm suggesting, and then throw me a text or leave me a message later so I know you're OK. I don't know if I'll be able to call later, but I'll definitely listen to messages and check texts. OK?"

Obviously, many calls will not be this easy. Try to stay calm and matter of fact to set the pace of the conversation.

These are some basic tips, as this book is not designed to teach you about actual counseling. This book is about the practical and business components. Counseling skills and methods will be covered in your certification program. As mentioned, most of these fundamentals are adequate for working at a facility, but they may not be enough for running a self-sustaining private practice. In this book's modalities sections, primers are provided to get you thinking and enhance your counseling skills, but they are just primers. The myriad of nuances and nearly infinite stream of perspectives you will need to transcend adequacy and become a powerful force of recovery and change are covered in *Project Addiction*. I fully admit that this reference is unabashed marketing and promotion, but I am confident that if you take a look at it, you will see it lives up to its title: *The Complete Guide to Using, Abusing, and Recovering from Drugs and Behaviors.*

This book, *Project Addiction Counselor*, was originally an afterthought: once I completed *Project Addiction*, I felt obligated and compelled to encourage individuals to go into private-practice recovery counseling. I am passionate about this needed shift in the field of addiction recovery. The addiction-recovery field needs to be populated by more private counselors, giving addicts options that work. The RIE gives the illusion of options, as there are hundreds of facilities to choose from, but they are far too similar; each one promotes itself as unique and innovative, but with my veteran addict (and counselor) eye, I see more similarities than differences. I search for, and never cease to be open to, the hope that there is a program that is innovative and unique to which I can refer clients who need inpatient treatment, but upon scrutiny I am always disappointed.

Appearance

The "Appearance" section provides detailed formulas for creating an appropriate appearance for those who might not have a natural ability for it, but it is important to emphasize and generalize here. Much of the drug culture is populated by disenfranchised, informal, and casual personalities. Many drug counselors feel it is appropriate to dress casually to avoid setting themselves far apart from the drug culture and ease bonding. This is incorrect and counterproductive. By acting and appearing like a mature and refined individual, you are setting an example of what is possible for everyone you work with. While bonding is important, so is making a motivating impression. I left my drug abuse in my past. Why would I deliberately keep the same—or similar—appearance I had in those times or in any times in the past? I don't dress the way I did when I was a child or play with building blocks anymore. I had a great time as a child, but that is in the past, and it is essential and liberating to reinvent myself. Until I am perfect, I want to know I am different each year of my life—more mature, refined, smarter, wiser—and my appearance should reflect that. I quit drugs so I could have access to all the things nonaddicts have, and this includes looking like a mature adult and a professional. If I am a mature adult and professional, my appearance should reflect that.

What to Wear

Should you wear a suit and tie? "Power" business dress? Sensible shoes? Jeans? A golf shirt? Loafers? The way we dress and put ourselves together is a form of expression. They say you cannot judge a book by its cover, but I do not agree. If a book is titled *Crazy Murderers on Rampage* and the cover depicts a bloody murder scene, it is safe to assume it is not a book of word-search puzzles!

Your appearance is an extension and expression of who you are. Your appearance must be comfortable enough for you not to feel awkward, yet not so comfortable that clients are not sure whether they're at a counseling session or a birthday barbecue!

Attempting to bond with addiction clients or youth can be tempting. However, if I meet with my banker or investment broker, I feel less confident if she's in flip-flops. We must dress for the role we are in. A mechanic wears a uniform, and so should you. It is recommended to design an appearance that looks casual yet professional. We want to look *nice*: well put together, matching, well groomed, and wrinkle-free! Below are some guidelines.

- No sneakers or sports shoes
- No jeans
- No shorts
- No miniskirts
- No sexy outfits
- No shorts (in case you didn't get it the first time)

You get the idea: no shorts. Ever. You're not coaching baseball; you're advising and mentoring.

Wear shoes that are comfortable but still appropriate for an office or as dress shoes.

Wear slacks, not jeans. Wear midlength or long skirts, but not sexy: we want the focus to be on the issues and the dialogue, not our biceps, triceps, calves, or thighs. Everyone is distracted by sex appeal. They may be attracted, threatened, or repelled, but almost never indifferent. You are not in session to get validation by subtly soliciting attention. Your appearance should express that you're a professional, but not as a banker! We are in the helping field, but we are not bound by tweed. If it looks good on you, that's a good choice, but if it doesn't, then don't wear it.

It takes trial and error to find and create the right look. As an intern, I was in such casual dress that I was easily mistaken for a patient or client. In my first sessions in private practice, I looked like a business executive (more like a banker): I wore a shirt, a jacket, a belt, a tie, and shiny shoes. It was a good look, but it just wasn't me. Nor was it approachable: it was too formal. I felt slightly self-conscious. It took about a year for me to get comfortable enough to experiment with other wardrobe styles, and eventually I found the right look for me: slacks, a dress shirt with folded cuffs and no tie and the top button open. I like things that match. That's my preference. I created a look that looked nice and organized and yet was not too powerful or dominating. I want the focus to be on my words, not my tie (but I miss my ties—I got some great ties).

Looking disheveled and odd is distracting, and so is looking perfect! What a contradiction! Can't win for losin'! Look nice. Look smart. Look well put together.

If you want clients to admire and respect you, you must exhibit admirable and respectful qualities. We cannot expect clients to do as we say and not as we do. If I plead with clients to be organized and focused, I must not only act that way, but my personal appearance and office environment must demonstrate those qualities as well.

Well groomed

Don't smell good, don't smell bad—don't smell like anything! Try to stay fit and eat and sleep right. I would never go to a dentist who'd lost all his teeth to poor care or a fitness trainer who was out of shape. Nor would I see a hairstylist who had a bad haircut! You need to inspire your clients by being the example for them. Be the best version of yourself you can be.

You are not required to be gorgeous or supermodel fit. Do the best with what you have and who you are—no excuses! You cannot accept excuses from addicts when they justify using, and if you do not live by what you teach and advise, you will be perceived as hypocritical. Practicing what you preach is critical in your role and is a serious responsibility. By living by what you advise, you inspire others by example. This is the best service you can provide. It isn't necessary to point out your lifestyle examples. Your good example will be subtly perceived; the same applies if you are hypocritical. Addict clients already feel the world is a foreign place they do not belong in, and it's our job to show them that if we can do it, they can, too.

So many clients can truly relate to me. I am the real deal: I authentically lived the life of a dope fiend, and clients cannot believe anything less when they hear me elucidate on it. You can't invent the subtle accuracies of the drug life I know. Yet I seem apart from that life. I look like a mature and professional, businessperson, so my presence exemplifies the possibilities open to my clients. Yes, these arms—beneath the nice shirt with folded cuffs—used to have heavy track marks. I'm both: an accomplished professional by conventional standards and a former dope fiend, too.

Tolerance

Addict clients will test you more than other clients. Because of their presenting issue, they are not in a responsible state of living. Unreliable behavior, tardiness, poor attendance, and poor commitment to treatment are all symptoms of this particular issue. It is necessary to develop the ability to depersonalize these behaviors and not judge too harshly or discontinue service for those who exhibit frustrating qualities. If you're going to discontinue work with every drug-issue client who is late or unreliable, you will not have very many clients to work with!

11

HYPNOTHERAPY

Hypnotherapy versus Hypnosis

Hypnosis is an artificially induced state of mind. Hypnotherapy is a therapeutic modality. Hypnosis is done on a stage, to entertain. Hypnotherapy is done in a therapeutic environment for self-improvement[12].

There are hundreds of hypnotherapy training programs, seminars, and schools to choose from. Most of them include a certification upon completion. Many of them offer weekend courses and seminars: if you pay a registration fee, book a room, and attend one or two intense four- to six-hour presentations over a weekend, you can receive their certification. If it sounds easy, that's because it is. Anyone can legally advertise and offer hypnotherapy, charge money for it, and provide it. There is no government regulating agency for this profession.

As previously mentioned, it is considered an avocational service and cannot be promoted as medical or clinical. Absolutely anyone can declare himself or herself a certified hypnotherapist. Absolutely anyone can legally offer and sell hypnotherapy certification and charge money for it. You could even create and print your own certificate, post it on your wall, and lead others to believe you went through rigorous training and are highly qualified.

---

[12]Hypnotherapy is not a required modality to create and sustain a private recovery practice. Regardless of whether you choose to use this modality in your practice, it is recommended that you read this section for other relevant, relatable practice ideas and benefits.

This is not recommended, however. Hypnotherapy is a powerful modality and can be highly effective when the practitioner is well trained.

Selecting Training

The first step to considering hypnotherapy training is to view the practice itself to see if it is a modality you feel has merit and can be useful to you. Browsing books and videos online will trigger a reaction: you will either be drawn to it or repelled. If you are drawn to it, continue to research and learn more about it. If you feel it is a useful modality for you, it is time to consider formal training. If you are not drawn to it, do not spend valuable time training for a modality you will not apply enthusiastically.

I have evaluated dozens of hypnotherapy programs (workshops and seminars) and found most to be rudimentary: lots of flash and pizzazz but little usable long-term substance. Some potential clients will ask about your credentials and where you trained. They may lose confidence in your skills if they look up your school and find it was a weekend seminar. Most who ask, however, will be satisfied with any answer you give and not check at all. The majority of clients seeking hypnotherapy are looking for assistance with weight loss, smoking cessation, or other common behavior modifications. Most hypnotherapy courses will cover these behaviors and train you to provide remedy for them.

However, you may eventually have the responsibility to serve someone with much more serious issues, like trichotillomania (hair pulling) or a driving phobia. Within six months of my practice even these behaviors were pedestrian, as I had pleas to help with everything from severe OCD to alcoholism. One man who contacted me had slowly developed agoraphobia (fear of public and/or open spaces). He was imprisoned in his home, immobilized by acute and severe feelings of terror. He had lost his job of twenty years and lost contact with all of his friends. His wife was at her wit's end and was considering leaving him. High-quality training, not a weekend seminar, qualified me to help him. After four months of weekly sessions—provided at his home—he was able to return to work and drive on the freeway.

We live in an age and culture that is conditioned to seek, and believe in shortcuts—quick - fixes to issues and problems. You may get contacted regularly to "cure" severe issues such as drug addiction or anorexia with hypnotherapy. Desperation can facilitate denial mechanisms, enabling people to believe that a session of hypnosis can cure such serious issues. If hypnotherapy were capable of such things, it would be a panacea. Hypnotherapy would be a billion-dollar industry, I'd be retired, having charged a million dollars per miracle session, and everyone on the planet would be perfect. The optimism of those clients who believe they can be cured by hypnotherapy is inspiring, but they need to be gently brought down to earth to see the realities of disorders and defects. Miracles can happen, but not the likes of the parting of the Red Sea.

It is easy to convince ourselves that the worst we can do is nothing, since hypnotherapy cannot hurt anyone in any way. However, when someone is searching desperately for relief from a debilitating behavior (such as the man who was twenty-four and terrified of driving a car), wasting their time for no results can erode hope and willingness to even attempt to seek and work on solutions for improvement. I've met many clients who said they had tried everything before they came to me and were on the cusp of giving up. That responsibility was a powerful motivator, and I felt obligated to either make a difference or advise them to seek another professional or another form of treatment. Their desperation motivated me to work harder, think deeper, and research and prepare to try to save them. It also humbled me to the point of selfless honesty. My bottom line was not worth a guilty conscience.

You must stay within your scope and range, no matter what. Over time, if your reputation is one of honesty, people will respect your willingness to put client welfare before profit, which will result in referrals. Don't take on an issue you cannot serve. Refer clients with such issues to someone, or at least admit to them that though you wish you could help, you cannot. Here is an example:

A forty-seven-year-old man came to me with a severe sleep disorder. With prescription medications, he was able to get to sleep, but he was routinely awakened by intense tinnitus (ringing in the ears). This condition caused him to take medical leave from his career as an airline pilot.

"I don't know if hypnotherapy can help your tinnitus. Since we spoke on the phone, I have studied many potential treatments. It looks unlikely that we will see much of a difference, as there is no evidence that tinnitus can be affected by hypnotherapy. I feel obligated to tell you the truth of the matter so you can decide to risk the expense or not. I will work hard to try to resolve the issue, and if at any time you feel this is not worth the expense, please don't hesitate to cancel."

He appreciated my honesty and willingness to try, and we began. After six sessions of hypnotherapy, his tinnitus was not affected at all. In each session I also provided hypnotic suggestions for sleep improvement, which yielded mild results. Over the few months we worked together, we developed a good rapport, and I also functioned as a life coach to him. Though I was totally unsuccessful in treating his tinnitus, he has remained a client for over seven years. His tinnitus has not improved at all, despite the thousands he has spent on devices, medications, and medical procedures, and his sleep remains so severely impacted that he has not been able to return to piloting.

This is an example of how doing the right thing pays more than doing the wrong thing. If I'd given him false expectations about hypnotherapy, he not only would've discontinued sessions once he realized I was not able to improve his condition, but he also would've never seen me—or referred me—again. He's done both. I provide approximately fifteen to twenty sessions per year for him.

Stay within Your Scope

A hypnotherapist cannot legally treat a disorder, such as OCD or ADD. However, a hypnotherapist can provide avocational service—a harmless and nonclinical modality of self-improvement.

The important thing is to stay within your comfort zone and scope; do not promote things you cannot deliver. The first time a client with OCD came to me in desperation, I disclaimed hypnotherapy, making sure the family realized it was an avocational form of self-improvement, not a treatment.

"I will try to help all I can," I told them, "but please be aware this is not a medical procedure or treatment. It may make a difference, and if we all try hard, it could be significant. If it doesn't, this will be apparent within a few sessions, and we'll terminate so as to not waste time, energy, hope, or your money."

The family confessed that they had already been to a battery of physicians and run the gamut of medications. Nothing had improved, and they felt they had nothing to lose.

"You've been through a lot," I replied. "I know it seems you have nothing to lose, but I will not take advantage of that, and you should be careful no one else does, either. No matter how bad something is, it can always be worse. We always have something to lose. Therefore, all I can do is my very best and be sincerely honest with you if I do not see this helping. If it is impossible to improve the situation, then time, energy, and resources will need to be redirected toward compensating for the disorder's effects and learning to adjust as best you can."

I was nervous. I felt a tremendous responsibility to help this young man. It seemed out of my scope and training, yet I was very willing to try, so long as they accepted my honest disclaimers. What if I *could* help this young man? If I was capable of assisting with OCD, I needed to find out. I had no proof it was out of my scope, as I had never tried. If I had tried helping OCD sufferers before and had failed, I would not even have considered working with him.

I insisted that he maintain his relationship with his psychiatrist and required his doctor's signature on a waiver. Only then did I administer hypnotherapy as a helping modality, and only in conjunction with the strategies his doctor prescribed along with the ones I designed and his doctor approved. Prior to this case, I had a very elementary understanding of OCD. When I agreed to work the case, I studied and devoured as much material as I could access on OCD as quickly as I could. Within two weeks, I had consumed volumes of material. If I was going to fail, it would not be through ignorance or a lack of trying.

That young man made tremendous progress. He has learned to manage his OCD, and his OCD meds were reduced as a result of his cognitive work. He received very beneficial treatment, and I became something of an expert on OCD—a win-win situation.

If you suspect an issue is beyond your scope to help, provide disclaimers and agree to experiment with hypnotherapy, but if after three to four sessions, no progress is made, service should be discontinued.

If you feel a client's issue is beyond your skill or scope you must deny assistance. When a family approached me to help with their son's schizophrenia and psychotic delusions, I told them those issues were beyond hypnotherapy and life coaching. "You need to be with a psychiatrist, and I recommend seeking one that specializes in this set of issues. With medication and treatment, this issue may become manageable, but there is no cure for this severe disorder. I am very willing to work with your whole family to help manage the dynamics of this disorder—and with your son, too—but it is vital that you understand and accept the limitations. Many psychiatric disorders are lifelong pathologies and will need care and attention throughout life, varying in intensity from time to time. I can advise you on how to manage and cope better, but I cannot impact the disorder itself any more than I can make a crippled person walk again. I can help your son cope and come to terms with his limitations and even help him toward a fulfilling life within the limitations of his disability, but I cannot heal his disability."

Hypnotherapy as an Enhancement

Hypnotherapy is an enhancement to cognitive work, not a replacement. I insist my clients do cognitive work. You cannot hypnotize issues away. Exercise, including cardiovascular exercise, and a proper diet are required to lose weight and become fit. Hypnotherapy can enhance the confidence and commitment needed to maintain these better behaviors, but it cannot make fitness appear or unwanted weight disappear. Enhanced confidence and commitment improve discipline, permitting someone to work out better, perform cardio more frequently, and sustain healthy eating choices. It is the working out, cardio, and proper diet that cause weight loss—hypnotherapy simply enhances the commitment and work.

It is the cognitive work and strategies applied that get results. Hypnotherapy enhances someone's ability to commit to the cognitive work and sustain it.

Training Recommendation

This is not a paid endorsement.

I recommend the Hypnosis Motivation Institute (HMI), founded by John Kappas (now deceased). Aside from Milton Erickson, no one has revolutionized hypnotherapy and hypnosis as much as Kappas. The HMI college is accredited and thorough. HMI provides extensive, detailed, thorough training on how to perform hypnotic induction and how to apply the techniques to specific issues. The institute has a full-time campus facility, classrooms, and ongoing classes and specialty courses, along with a distance-learning program.

This books chapter, "Select Training" will give you guidelines on how to research and select a course.

I also recommend having a copy of the *Handbook of Hypnotic Suggestions and Metaphors*, edited by D. Corydon Hammond, PhD. In addition, I recommend studying Milton Erickson. There are many books on him and about him. Unfortunately, Erickson himself did not author a book. Ernest L. Rossi has compiled and edited many of Erikson's speeches and interviews to provide the best possible account of his work.

Erickson could never describe his own methods, as he was extraordinarily intuitive. His methods were very spontaneous. While many have dissected and analyzed Erickson's methods, I do not believe anyone has ever been able to put an applicable, structured formula to his work. Neurolinguistic programming (NLP) promotes itself as an Ericksonian modality.

NLP is interesting and can be very effective in the right circumstances; however, when someone uses NLP around or on me, I am immediately resistant and feel condescended to. When I was exposed to NLP as a modality, I recognized it as something I had been exposed to many times before. I dub it the "used-car salesman" technique. While it is highly effective on those who are suggestible to it, it is repellent to those who are not.

Neurolinguistic Programming

Neurolingusitic programming (NLP) was created by Richard Bandler and John Grinder in California in the 1970s. NLP theory is based in the concept of leading people to draw conclusions through subtle physical movements and language choices (e.g., intonations, emphasis, and "punch" words that create subconscious associations). Look up "yes-set/NLP" online, and you'll get an idea of how it works. I feel that 50 percent of the hypnotherapy community considers it effective and insightful while the other 50 percent finds it bogus. While NLP has never worked on me, I've seen some very talented NLP practitioners use it effectively as a tool for persuasion in sales and even in therapy.

NLP can be a powerful tool when used on individuals who are suggestible to it, but it can be intensely counterproductive on those who aren't. I am confident there are NLP masters who can adapt NLP to nearly any person or situation. It is never easy to be a master at anything. An NLP practitioner should be proficient in determining who is suggestible to it and who is not and apply it accordingly. An NLP practitioner should become an expert on suggestibility types, knowing whom NLP can be useful with while mastering the techniques themselves—in that order.

If this practice interests you, you should develop your NLP skills and learn when and to whom to apply it. Do not rely on it as your main modality. It is one of many tools to use.

HMI—John Kappas

HMI is the only hypnosis college accredited by the Accrediting Council for Continuing Education and Training (ACCET).

When visiting the council's website, you will see an extensive list of agencies, unions, and associations that recognize and accept HMI. Some, but certainly not all, of these were founded and invented by HMI. The Hypnotherapist's Union Local 472 was founded and created by HMI, as was the American Hypnosis Association (AHA).

Being able to include AHA and Local 472 on your hypnotherapist business cards and websites increases your credibility and is a powerful marketing tool. HMI's distance-learning course taught me not only proficiency in hypnotherapy, but it also showed me how to treat dozens of presenting issues, how to use versatile helping modalities, and how to establish a hypnotherapy practice and marketing. It is a thorough course that teaches students how to counsel and advise clients, one that I feel rivals any university course and surpasses many.

The cornerstone of the HMI program is Kappas's Emotional/Physical Personality Theory (E&P), in which the entire spectrum of personality is distilled into two distinct personalities, the emotional (introvert) and the physical (extrovert). Knowledge of E&P theory makes one an insightful and powerful hypnotherapist who can get results when no one else can. Hypnotherapy was once considered only applicable to "hypnotically suggestible" people, and it was generally accepted that only 30 percent of the population was hypnotically suggestible. But E&P shows hypnotherapists how to determine someone's suggestibility type, making hypnotherapy applicable to 100 percent of the population. Kappas discovered that *all* people are hypnotically suggestible if you apply the correct style of suggestion. He found that there was an entire type of hypnotic suggestion never before considered and that another 30 to 40 percent of the population was suggestible to it. Once he discovered this, he developed ways to determine which type of suggestibility a person has so the practitioner can apply the correct type. Erickson's ability to apply hypnotic techniques to nearly anyone and everyone was evidence that everyone can respond to suggestion. Kappas isolated and taught the different techniques.

Understanding E&P enhances your ability to communicate in the most effective manner based on a particular person's personality type, enabling you to sustain long-term client relationships.[13] It teaches you how to adapt techniques to your clients rather than using techniques that get them to adapt to you (NLP style). Not only does E&P make you a more effective therapist, counselor, friend, spouse, partner, and so on ad infinitum, but when you introduce E&P theory to clients, they are intrigued and often want to learn more of it and how to apply it in their own lives, whether in business or in parental and spousal relationships. Many of my clients requested sessions just to learn more about E&P and how to apply it. I would often provide E&P literature for them to study, but sessions were required to show them how to better apply it in real life. A large bulk of my revenue from life coaching and hypnotherapy is due to teaching (and using) E&P.

A counselor should never infer that a client has issues where none exist. Counselors should be versatile and able to offer real assistance in as many areas of life as they can. Introducing E&P as a way of maximizing personal relationships with spouses, friends, kids, parents, and anyone on the planet intrigues clients and provides observable results for them. A three- to four-session issue can evolve into four to six months of counseling and coaching, as people are drawn to E&P, finding it so useful they often want to master it.

Shoulders of Giants

Kappas confesses to have stood on the shoulders of giants such as Erickson, Freud, and others and expanded or refined their works to offer new perspectives, as did Carl Jung, the protégé of Freud. Freud is indeed the father of psychoanalysis. But his protégé, Jung, was able to expand and refine the foundations of psychotherapy to develop powerful methods that incorporated mythology, the subconscious archetype, and other deep concepts. Many

---

[13] *Relationship Strategies: The E&P Attraction* is the book Kappas wrote on the theory. I personally do not feel his own book does the theory justice. The classes, workshops, and presentations on the subject elaborate further, and I feel both are critical to one's ability to use E&P effectively.

people fall into one camp or the other, Freud or Jung. I am a Jungian, but I'm not opposed to Freudian psychology. Jungian psychology only exists because of Freud. I do not apply Freudian techniques for the same reason I don't read by candlelight. Candlelight is perfect and certainly not flawed, but I have electric light now, so I use a better version.

Just as Kappas refined and evolved his predecessors' works and theories, I have found ways to apply E&P that are more effective and comprehensive than what I was taught by HMI. Over time, you also will expand your learned modalities to develop your own style and methods.

As a professional, you must develop your own styles and refine every modality you use to suit your own strengths and weaknesses and to adapt to your clients.

HMI

I completed the HMI distance-learning course in 1999. It cost approximately $3,000 and required about three months of intense commitment. I watched one to three sixty- to ninety-minute DVD classes per day, studied the accompanying written materials, and completed the exams, e-mailing them to the institute for grading. Training was thorough and extensive, and I had access to the school's instructors (via phone, e-mail, or appointment) and the on-site library. Some prefer to attend school in person. While I lived near enough to the HMI location (forty minutes away), I was a full-time parent and the owner of a construction company, which made it impractical for me to attend in person. Personally I prefer to work at my own pace. A six-month program took me three. I am a better student from a book than I am in a classroom.

We all must know our learning style. Some are better at (and require) classroom environments with live instruction while others require being on their own. Neither is better or worse. The only mistake that can be made is underestimating or overestimating your ability in either format. Everyone has an innate learning style—classroom or solo—and must choose which one works better for him or her. I fail miserably in classrooms, but I excel on my own; others fail on their own but excel in classrooms.

Distance learning is usually a hybrid: you study from home (if you're in another state, city, or country), but you attend virtual classes by DVD or online videos. HMI's video classes were filmed live in the eighties and packaged (the fashion is classic!). While you can't raise your hand and ask a question, you do get the dynamism of an actual classroom and can make a list of questions to submit later to an instructor at the institute.

I also liked the opportunity to replay a class or segment that I struggled with. Having total access and command over the class was effective and often needed.

You can go to the HMI website to review. It is a program I believe in, and my role in this book is to provide readers with actual, workable strategies for success. I only teach through verified experience, not theoretical. Many hypnotherapy courses may be very effective; however, I simply cannot verify them as good (or bad).

I began my practice as a hypnotherapist hoping it would be a full career. Over time, I found that there are not enough hypnotherapy clients to sustain a lucrative full-time career. I do not recommend it as a sole source of income. Very few hypnotherapists are able to sustain a career without offering other modalities. Between hypnotherapy clients, life-coaching clients, and addiction-recovery clients, I was able to sustain twenty to thirty clients per week. Hypnotherapy was approximately 25 percent, life coaching was about 25 percent, and addiction recovery was easily 50 percent, sometimes more.

Student Exercise

- Browse Amazon for books on hypnotherapy, and read any samples that are available.
- Do basic online research into the subject.
- View YouTube videos.

12

LIFE COACH

There are no legal requirements or licensing to be a life coach. No government agencies regulate the field. So long as you do not step into the territory of treatment or clinical care, it is legal and safe to provide life-coaching services.

Absolutely anyone can be a life coach and proclaim to be one. I never attended formal life-coach training. My hypnotherapy practice slowly evolved into a life-coaching practice. I discovered that many of my clients were referring to me as their life coach, and many sessions no longer included hypnotherapy, as many clients preferred to spend the session discussing their issues and have me advise them.

After about a year of being referred to as a life coach, I adopted the title.

I am not recommending this approach. I have a knack and developed some talent for this modality. Most people think they are naturals at counseling, and while many are right, just as many are wrong. It is important to put emphasis on the fact that clients dubbed me a life coach long before I self-proclaimed it. I did not unilaterally proclaim myself as a life coach. Please don't confuse my intent: by informing you that a license or certification is not legally required, I am not advocating bypassing it. Nor am I discouraging a certification process. I am trying to relay all the relevant information in order to empower you to make your own decision. I truly believe only the strong will survive: the ones who get results helping others will sustain a practice, and those who don't will not. Formal training and certification may make the difference in skill and proficiency.

If you provide life-coaching services without training and do not get results or maintain clients with that service, you should seriously consider formal training. While I did not attend a formal life-coach training program, I did study the field extensively on my own. I am a voracious reader. Studying therapy, psychology, and other helping modalities has been a passion of mine throughout adulthood, and I would wager that much of my self-study rivals the content of many university courses.

Selecting Training

As far as I'm aware, there is nothing other than seminar-style programs for life-coach training. Many of them are held in conference rooms at hotels near airports, some are conducted online only, and many are a combination of the two.

I have searched online for available life-coach training sources and found dozens throughout the world. The information available on their websites is basic and self-promoting. Some provide costs, dates, and locations of training, but many do not. The ones that do not provide that information encourage calling for more information. I phoned seven different programs and only got voicemails that asked me to leave my contact information for a callback. I am skeptical about any profession that conceals its information unless I provide mine first. If they have confidence in what they provide, the information would be up-front and accessible. Forcing people to call to gain basic information seems a ploy for a salesperson to gain access to callers.

I was not willing to submit my personal information or participate in sales calls, which would likely open me up to an inundation of e-mails and calls from any and every agency the company wanted to sell my information to or share it with. No thanks.

My research showed that the average life-coach training program costs between $700 and $900 for three- or five-day programs in either seminar or webinar format.

In addition, there are many life-coach training books available. I recommend only ones that are from an established, credible source that allow you to review the topics they cover before you purchase them. Very few of the ones that are available fit these criteria. *Becoming a Professional Life Coach: Lessons from the Institute of Life Coach Training* seems to be a credible source. It covers important topics and seems to be written well. However, since I have not read it, I cannot offer you a review.

Versatility

A life coach must be versatile.

You should be able to adapt to not only the many different issues you'll be presented with, but also the personalities of those who present them. Everyone is different, and it is not the client who must adapt to you—you must adapt to the client.

A huge challenge is to be able to adapt to a personality that is fundamentally different from yours while still maintaining your own individual personality to not compromise authenticity. You must maintain your own character while not threatening anyone else's. People feel threatened if they perceive you as different, unusual, better, or even worse than they are. Everyone is more comfortable and accepting with those who are similar to themselves. Most clients can be accepting of other's differences, so long as those differences are not offensive. Everyone is repelled by an individual who is inauthentic. It takes time and experience to craft the skill of adapting to other people while still maintaining your own authenticity. The subject of authenticity is elaborated on in the section about working with minors.

Never compromise who you are, but never appear judgmental, critical, or superior to others.

Below is an example:

I live in a predominantly omnivorous and Christian society in the United States, which makes me a minority: I am a vegetarian and adhere more to Eastern spirituality and philosophy than Western. I would never lie about my religious beliefs or dietary preferences, but I don't advertise them, either. While most people respect my values, many may not. Many conservative omnivores feel threatened by my values, and I respect that. My values are not conventional, and people tend to fear what they do not know.

Clients who know me well and have for some time know many personal things about me, as I share openly to establish trust and rapport: I cannot expect strangers to be open with me without being open with them. Some of these clients may not agree with my lifestyle choices, but they are accepting and respectful of them.

While I would never lie about my dietary or religious choices, I am discreet about them.

Some of the best spiritual discussions and counseling I've had were with a highly conservative Mormon. I am a Bhakti-Hindu (considered liberal), and he was a Mormon (considered conservative). We had one paramount thing in common: our faith and devotion to God. Religion was not a topic of conversation when we were first getting acquainted, but it provided hours of discussion once we knew and respected each other as men, husbands, and fathers.

Our differences, even good ones, can cause disharmony and threaten rapport with a client, and without rapport we will not be accepted as an adviser.

I must live by high standards and values effectively if I am to back up advice by self-verified example. I must also be sure to respect others' differences.

It is essential to find the common ground with a client. We all have something in common. This may be kids, work, financial concerns, or health concerns. The greatest common ground we have as people is simple: we all want to be loved, feel fulfilled, be comfortable, and be free of fear. Be open and honest with discretion about who are and look for common areas to bond over.

Client Commitment Equals Client Results

Results require commitment. Without true commitment, effort is minimal. If effort is minimal, results are compromised.

Get your clients to commit to the strategies you provide by closing off exits and anticipating excuses so they follow through.

Say, for example, that a client's commitment to exercise two days per week is ambiguous. Which two days? What time on those days, and for how long? What type of workout? These details need to be filled in. The subconscious is adept at avoidance. This is how exercise (or any good habit) is neglected to begin with. If you detail the actual commitment with the client, a new behavior becomes more concrete and actual and no longer ambiguous. Get your clients to make appointments for their new behaviors (e.g., exercise is on Tuesdays and Thursdays for one hour after dinner).

Clients will appreciate your assertiveness if it is not expressed in a condescending or commanding tone. As the coach, you must box clients in to a new discipline, reminding them that good habits are created the same way bad ones are: through repetition. Get your clients to become dependent on a new behavior, the same way they've become dependent on a bad one.

The subconscious will always attempt to sabotage new behaviors—even good ones—making so-called exit-closed strategies the best. An exit-closed strategy is one that is detailed, including time, place, what, how, and how long. An ambiguous strategy lacks details, relying on vague terms like *whenever, later, soon, a lot,* and *a little.* These words are far too open to interpretation, and the sabotaging subconscious will interpret them as excuses to procrastinate.

Deductive Reasoning

A coach is to advise and suggest, not to command. Deductive reasoning without judgment prevents clients from feeling intimidated or threatened. Deductive reasoning is the process of narrowing an idea or plan to its simplest and most logical conclusion. We systematically deduct, subtract, and eliminate elements that are not productive or counterproductive until only the sensible and productive remain. Ease your clients into submission—don't force! This is explained further in "Counseling Modalities".

Coaching and advising can be done in a conversational tone. A session should not feel like a board meeting or a doctor's visit. Nor should it feel like hanging out with friends. The former is too clinical while the latter is too informal, and neither will foster commitments needed for results.

You are not a friend to your clients. You are their coach or counselor. Be friendly, but maintain an authoritarian role. Your role is one of an advisor and coach, not a buddy. Buddies are free, and you charge a fee for your time—as well you should. Maintain your role: that of a friendly yet authoritarian mentor.

The need to be versatile is reemphasized here. Be social and friendly with clients, especially the ones under twenty-five who do not respond well to a formal dynamic. Be social and informal, goof around and have casual conversation, but never abandon the role of a coach. Hone the skill of being able to switch into coach mode in an instant without seeming bipolar.

Transitions from the informal to the formal should seem seamless. You might say, "So, anyway, to be serious about the issue," and reassert the issue you're working on. Clients may resist, seeming to prefer that you spend time with them in a more casual and informal manner. It's their time and money, so what's the harm?

It will hurt your practice—that's the harm. That client may grow to like you, but he or she is not gaining anything for his or her time and money spent. Every session should include advice, insight, or homework.[14] If a client's friends ask what he or she learned or gained from your last session, he or she should be able to give an answer. After every session, ask yourself what you taught or revealed for your client, and if you cannot answer, you failed in that session. Some sessions do take on a frivolous, informal texture, but it is your job to be sure your client walks away with something he or she can use. It's up to the client to use it, but it's up to you to provide it.

As you explore a relevant issue, some clients may change the subject to more casual and frivolous topics that have nothing to do with the issues to be discussed. Before you realize it, ten to fifteen minutes can be used up. While it is rude to ignore or blatantly dismiss frivolous comments or conversation, it is your responsibility to keep the session on track. The mind has defense mechanisms, and some clients will use casual topics as an avoidance tool. These need to be neutralized artfully and effectively.

Case Conference

Jake is twenty-four and immature for his age, and he lacks motivation. He is not a self-starter and often procrastinates. Our sessions always begin informally: "Hey, Jake. Nice to see you, man. What's new?"

"Not much. Just saw somebody taking like eight minutes to park their car outside! It was funny!"

---

[14] *Homework* refers to cognitive-behavioral assignments to experiment with.

160

"Yeah, stupid drivers are everywhere! Sometimes it's you, and sometimes it's me!"

"I just wonder why the parking on this street is so bad for such a small neighborhood."

"Yeah, it bugs me, too. Seems there's gotta be a better system. But hey—tell me how that job interview went." If I do not redirect the conversation, Jake will use up a lot of time on these insignificant observations.

"It went well. The guy asked me..."

Jake would share the interview story but get sidetracked by irrelevant details: "This interviewer was wearing a purple and pink tie. Is that professional? I mean, it was distracting. Oh, his office had a great view, by the way."

I divert the sidetrack back to relevant issues: "So you think it went well? Great. What exactly did he ask? How did you answer? Do you feel you made a good impression? Is there anything you would do differently if you could do it again?" (Note that I did not take the bait to discuss ties, nor did I advise him to stay on relevant subjects.)

My replies are artfully designed to avoid the casual talk and reestablish focus without hitting a nerve: I do not comment on his avoidance at all, and I follow my comments with questions that force him to respond, engaging him in relevant dialogue.

Jake would comment on things out the window or get sidetracked by frivolous details every few minutes. Rather than remind him to stay focused, I would simply redirect the focus each time it was diverted. This is more economical and effective than talking about avoidance. I was conditioning him to be focused rather than asking him to be—showing, not telling.

Being Assertive

A common complaint among clients is about the so-called passive helping professional. The passive coach is someone who encourages the client to do the majority of the talking while asking only generic questions, such as "And how does that make you feel?" or "Well, what do *you* think *you* should do?" What clients are thinking when they hear these clichés is, "Gee, I dunno! Isn't that what I'm paying *you* for?"

Clients have taken their time and money to come and see a professional. It is your obligation to carry the burden of conversation, provide answers, and avoid awkward silences or pauses. Pauses and silent moments are a great way to place emphasis on a point, but they should not be long or awkward. They should be done artfully and placed strategically. It is not the client's responsibility to carry the conversations or think of relevant topics. The client is your guest, and the burden of filling the time and keeping the time poignant is on you. While many clients are very proactive in a session, others have trouble connecting to the topics and issues they want help with. It is your job to fish important issues out for them and find the areas of their lives that need attention.

Forty percent of clients will arrive at their sessions with topics to discuss and issues to address. Sixty percent of clients arrive with nothing to say. This is not intentional: they expect the expert to be attentive enough to initiate discussion of relevant things. If you have a client who really seems to have nothing on his or her mind, it is acceptable (and encouraged) to initiate a topic about life you feel may be relevant: "So I was thinking this morning about life's routines and how tough it can be to feel motivated to do the mundane, everyday things needed in life" You can then expand on the subject itself, asking a few questions along the way to invite the client into the topic: "What do you think?"

In this example, the topic is not specifically about the client or even a specific event or issue. It is about life in general. This lack of personalizing can neutralize awkwardness.

Initiating conversation and topics can be a huge burden, as very introverted clients can be shy. It is your responsibility to help them be comfortable enough to open up and converse.

Working with Introverts

When you work with introverted clients, do not point out how quiet they are, and never, ever say, "It's OK—don't be shy" or anything that draws attention to their awkwardness. Ease them into trusting you by not pointing out faults or defects. If you sense they are shy, pick up the conversational slack, and watch how an introvert can become very chatty!

Working with Extroverts

Likewise, do not point out that extroverts are very talkative and social: roll with their behavior by participating in the conversation, and slowly segue into being the dominant personality in the room. This is where NLP is effective: matching personality and subtly transitioning to an alternate pace. Allow the clients to be themselves by not calling attention to how they are or are not. Slowly dominate the session. It is essential to control the room. This should never be done aggressively or condescendingly, but slowly and assertively. No one should be able to identify the actual point of transfer or change of pace.

Ending a Session

It is awkward and clichéd to end a session with, "Well, our time is up." Closure must be subtle and implied. About ten minutes before time is up, look for a comfortable moment to opine or elucidate on whatever is currently being discussed. Begin with, "We've only got about ten minutes left, so let me comment on what you just told me" or, "Let me comment on something we talked about earlier before we're out of time. I want to be sure I address that topic."

This shows you were paying attention, provides a segue, and also brings up the need to prepare to wind things up. Thus the "time is up" idea is somewhat buried in the context of the topic to be addressed and does not stand out. It is a gentle and polite reminder, similar to something you might say to a visiting neighbor without being rude.

You should not look at your watch or clock in any observable way. In the examples above, the time has been mentioned, folded into the sentences.

13
SELECT TRAINING

When it comes to training, there are general guidelines to go by to ensure your time and money is smartly applied, regardless of whether the modality is hypnotherapy, life coaching, or a cooking class.

For life coaching and hypnotherapy, there are dozens of training opportunities in every major city in the United States and abroad, but most of them are not worth the investment, so be careful. Good salesmanship can make a program seem essential, so scrutinize and vet each program. Don't know what questions to ask? Below is a list to get you started. As you call and speak to a few programs, other questions and concerns will arise in your mind. Add those to the list of inquiries.

- Tell me about your program.
    - o Allow the salesperson to give you the basics and initiate concerns. Tell him or her that you're shopping and taking notes.
    - o Take notes.
- What does your training cost?
- How long is the program?
- Where does it take place?
- What type of materials will I need? (Books? Papers? Apps? Software?)
    - o Are these materials provided or in addition to the overall cost?
- Is my registration fee refundable if I change my mind? What if I'm unsatisfied?
    - o What are the refund policies?

- What does the program cover?
  - Marketing? Running a practice?
  - Certification?
    - What does the certification legally permit me to do?
    - What am I not permitted to do?

Hypnotherapy Training

  - What type of inductions are taught?
  - How many types of inductions are taught?
  - Does the program teach about suggestibility?
    - What does it teach about suggestibility?
  - How many hypnotic styles will be taught?
  - Are specific issues taught?
    - Are smoking cessation, weight loss, confidence, and nail biting covered?

Life-Coach Training

  - What areas of coaching are specifically covered?
  - Is building rapport covered? If so, how?
  - Marketing?

Drug Counseling (refer to the "Addiction Counseling" section of this book)

  - What is the cost?
  - How many hours (or units) are required?
  - Does the program provide or facilitate the state's exam?
  - Are continuing-education units available?
  - How does the CEU program work?
  - Is the course online, on campus, or both?
  - What topics are covered?

You should rank your questions in order of importance.

Is cost of the training the highest priority? You must be frugal, but not so conservative that you accept inadequate training. Bad training can be worse than none.

What about location? Timing? Scheduling?

Which questions are the most decisive for you? If timing and availability is the most significant, rank it first. If cost is second most vital, rank it second.

Create a training file to document all of your research data. Your file should have subfiles for each modality (hypnotherapy, life coaching, addiction, yoga).Take notes, and file them in your newly created file for comparison and analysis. If anyone tells you that signing up now will be less expensive or gives you other incentives to rush your decision, insist that the discount and incentive be included regardless of when you sign up. Do not fall prey to pressure sales.

After you've interviewed four to seven training centers, go through your file. Some of them will go straight into the trash. The ones that have potential should be scored: rate every answered question between one and five, and add up the total score.

As you rank the questions and answers, you will get a clearer sense of the more appropriate choice. Contact the top three courses again, and interview them again. Try to talk to a different salesperson in order to sense inconsistencies.

Once you've completed your scoring analysis, set it aside. Pick it up again in a few days, and review the material. Do you feel the same? Consistency is key. As time passes, we generally feel better about a right choice—not the same, and certainly not worse. If you feel consistently indecisive about a program, your intuition is speaking.

Once you've sifted down the options to the best pick, make contact again, and interview them one more time. Wait for the data to settle in your mind for two or three days before handing over your money and time. By now your intuitive sense is based in logic, reason, intellect, imagination, and vision and can be trusted.

Once you've registered and paid your deposit or tuition and refund deadlines are in the past, there is no turning back. Trust that you made an intelligent decision that was smartly evaluated. If you did make a mistake, there was not much more you could have done to avoid it, so apply yourself to the program, and make it work.

Harvard does not create good lawyers, and Princeton does not create great doctors. These universities provide a stellar education and all the knowledge needed to be good at these professions, but it is the student who exploits that knowledge to become successful.

You will need to exploit the training and knowledge you're given and transfer it into practical use. This book should help. The rest is up to you.

I do not recommend weekend seminars or workshops for hypnotherapy. It is my opinion that they are rapid downloads of basic information that is usually accessible from the Internet and books. Both online and print mediums can be accessed multiple times at your leisure, but it is nearly impossible to retain sufficient information from a workshop or seminar. If you wish to review workshop information, most providers offer refresher courses for a fee. This is a very good marketing strategy to get customers to pay twice for the same information.

If you are attending a conference, workshop, or seminar, invest about $100 in a digital recorder that will download the recorded content from a flash drive to your tablet or hard drive: an inexpensive alternative to a refresher course.

After you've completed a course, it is good to augment the training with other studies on the subject. Studying from other resources during a course, however, may impede your focus and interfere with the matter you are learning and being provided. Therefore, it is best to wait until the program is completed to augment your studies.

14

ALTERNATIVE MODALITIES

Any modality that is not conventional to the medical and insurance industries is categorized as alternative. Hypnotherapy and life coaching are two such modalities. There are many psychiatrists who practice hypnotherapy and many therapists and psychologists who are also life coaches, but these are not considered prime or conventional modalities.

Yoga, acupuncture, Ayurvedic medicine, nutrition, meditation, fitness, energy healing, and any other helping modality that you feel is valuable can augment your practice and give you areas to specialize in. Any modality you're trained in or experienced in can be folded into your practice and marketed. If you are not certified or trained in a modality but would like to be, add it to your list of needed certifications. The ones included in this book are optional as well. It is certainly possible to create and sustain a private practice with only addiction-counseling services (or hypnotherapy or life coaching). It will be more challenging, to say the least, but it is possible, and the fact that there are a few of these solo-modality practices in existence proves it can be done.

The wider the variety of services you offer, the more accessible you are to your community. The more products and services you offer, the more clients you will maintain a relationship with for longer.

It is unwise to provide services only in conjunction with your alternative modalities. Offering a counseling program that is reliant upon yoga, fitness, or hypnotherapy may attract potential clients who have an understanding of and confidence in these specific modalities, but it will exempt you from sections of the population who are not and may only want counseling. To sustain a full practice, you cannot afford to deny clients who may not want to participate in a specific modality. As an addiction counselor and hypnotherapist, I offer hypnotherapy as a modality option to my addiction clients; it is not a requirement. There is no additional cost for it for anyone who wants it applied, and it requires only fifteen to twenty minutes of session time. Some addiction clients insist on the hypnotherapy service, and some want nothing to do with it. I offer it, and, depending on the response, perform it or leave it alone, never bringing it up again. If the client changes his or her mind and wants to know more or try it, he or she will ask, but it is rude and awkward for me to insist, regardless of how much I feel it would be an effective service for a particular client. I am not a hypnotherapist–addiction counselor; I am an addiction counselor *and* a hypnotherapist (and a life coach). Anyone can hire me for one modality exclusively or for combinations of them.

I recommend creating your practice with optional services. Once you become established and proficient in a modality, you can consider making it a central feature and possibly the core service. In the beginning, you can use alternative modalities to enhance service and clientele. As you mature in a specific modality, it will slowly emerge as a specialty. That is when you can decide to abandon other modalities or make it central to your services while still offering the other services.

Think of your alternative modality as a separate business, a service that stands alone but can also be used to augment any type of service someone has sought you out for.

Student Exercise

- What alternative modalities are you interested in?
- What alternative modalities are you trained in or proficient at?
- What would you like to offer and why?
- How would you apply it to synthesize and enhance other modalities?
- Research training for at least two other modalities.

Biofeedback

Biofeedback is used to improve health by causing physiological changes in conjunction with changes to thoughts and emotions. It is a tool used to gauge and monitor physiological functions such as brain waves, muscle tone, heart rate, and breathing through skin conductance. A conductive device is adhered to the client's skin, and this device transmits physiological readings to the controller, similar to an EKG heart monitor.

Biofeedback can be very effective, especially when combined with relaxation exercises and hypnotherapy. It is primarily used for stress management, but it can also stimulate imagination, creativity, reasoning function, coordination, and other functions.

I recommend Heartmath's biofeedback devices. Heartmath is a leader in biofeedback, and the company specializes exclusively in this technology and its benefits. It does not sell, promote, or associate with anything else. This exclusive commitment has made Heartmath a pioneer in this effective and growing helping modality.

Personally, I feel the Heartmath products easily rival the elaborate high-tech systems that cost thousands of dollars to purchase. Many biofeedback technicians charge top dollar for their services with these devices. While they do get results, I do not feel their results are substantially better than what they could achieve with the Heartmath equipment. The results these professionals get are due to their expertise more than the equipment. Their equipment is high tech and gives a powerful impression, which can add a placebo effect to the work. This is just my opinion, and I certainly do not mean to offend or undermine professionals in the biofeedback community. I have very limited exposure to and experience with the field, so my perception is limited.

I highly recommend adding biofeedback to your private-practice counseling. It enhances hypnotherapy and can be used as a stand-alone modality as well. I have placed ads promoting this service and received good response. When applicable, I've offered it to existing clients, all of whom have gotten much out of it and scheduled several additional sessions for just that treatment.

The Heartmath emWave Pro costs approximately $300 and comes with everything you need to run many treatments with it, including software and finger and ear sensors. The device is driven from your USB port. While a client is attached to the sensors, you can monitor the feedback live on your computer while instructing and guiding him or her through therapeutic exercises.

Heartmath also has an emWave2, which costs approximately $200 and is for personal use. It is a portable handheld device. I have provided these units to clients so they could continue with the biofeedback exercises and treatments outside of our appointments. I sell them at cost, simply facilitating the purchase and providing instruction on how to use the device. I do not feel it is necessary to make a profit from the device, which they could easily go online and buy on their own, since I am compensated for our sessions. Processing the order and instructing them how to use it helps strengthen rapport and aligns the device's use with our session work. Encouraging and assisting in its use is great marketing and a great service.

15

POLYMATHY

That title got your attention, huh? *Polymathy* sounds like some type of behavioral depravity, but a polymath is someone who is learned in many fields.

While it is important to be well informed in as many helping modalities as possible, you should also be well versed in general areas of knowledge: psychology, neurology, biology, religion, philosophy, and other sciences which are all integral to rapport and wide-spectrum servicing. The more subjects you can converse about, the greater spectrum of people you can relate to and help.

It is better to be somewhat knowledgeable in many things and an expert in nothing than to be an expert in one thing but ignorant to all others.

Yep, being a prolific *Wikipedia* reader is better than having read only one text cover to cover! Brush up, review, skim—look up *everything*. Anytime a subject grabs your interest, look into it further until you're satisfied. Make a list of topics that grab your attention, and every other week, review the list and examine the topics at your leisure. Make acquiring insights and useful information a hobby. It is easy to become entertained and pass the time with social media and TV, but with the same spare time, you can review and peruse different relevant topics and subjects. This can be done even while watching TV, or you can toggle back and forth between Facebook and Twitter and several websites about an interesting topic that is relevant to your role as a counselor and mentor. You do not need to sacrifice your time-passing hobbies, but conjoin them with mind-expanding materials.

Jobs come to a temporary close when the shift is over, but careers are ongoing. You should spend time each week researching, studying, or reviewing topics and subjects that may be relevant to your practice. And what isn't relevant? Here's my own formula: I read every night when I go to bed. The twenty to thirty minutes it takes for me to fall asleep are spent reading. Reading makes me tired and peaceful, so it's a good sleep aid, too. I am involved with two to four books at any given time. The time I spend reading in bed is divided: I usually spend ten to fifteen minutes on each book. I also have a book in the bathroom (c'mon, at least I admit it!), and anytime I'm required to wait for a doctor, wait at the DMV, or endure other boring waiting-room scenarios, I tote a book along. Like most people, I'm way too busy to have time dedicated to studying, so I use time that is useless, such as in waiting rooms. Reading can become habitual, and reading time can be split between books: entertainment (your favorite spy thriller or romance novel) and books of practicum (nonfiction topics that enhance your awareness and knowledge).

You do not need to be an expert in sports, sewing, or pop music. But by having basic—even rudimentary— knowledge in many areas, you can converse on many subjects. You never know when knowing about some subject may create a bond between you and a specific client. Having access to many areas of intellect also makes a very positive impression.

DVDs and other video media can be resources, too. When *The Secret* became a pop sensation, I made sure to view it. I thought it sucked, but at least when clients referenced it, I knew what the heck they were talking about! (If half of you just threw my book away because I said *The Secret* sucked, you probably don't want to know what I think of *Fifty Shades of Grey*.) Clients bring me books they are excited about, and if I read all of them, I would never get a chance to read my own selections. I graciously accept all suggestions and gifts and at least look them over. If a client is considerate enough to want to share something

175

with me, I will at least read enough of it to give an opinion and have a brief conversation about it. I thoroughly consume ones that are truly relevant to me (very few, unfortunately).

That being said, you should not advise your clients to read books *you* think are relevant. Clients should never feel pressured or obligated to read something or to even be interested. You can introduce the topic and reference a book you've read, giving a sentence or two of endorsement, but leave it at that. In my office I keep a few extra copies of books I feel strongly about so I can loan them out to any client who may be sincerely interested. Many people intend to buy a copy of a book you're discussing, but after the session, it is natural for everyday events to interfere with the errand to the bookstore or Amazon, so the recommendations are often not pursued for legitimate reasons of inconvenience—it's not personal. Few clients ever return the books, CDs or DVDs I loan, so I look at a loan as a gift. Of the DVDs I've loaned out, approximately 30 percent have been returned; as for the other 70 percent, I can rarely even remember whom I loaned them to. I used to make notes and even thought of having people sign them out, but I realized that would be tacky. I buy extra copies to share. (To save money, I often buy used copies in good conditions.)

I loan these materials when they are relevant to the progress of a client, not simply for entertainment. You're not a video store or a library—you're a counselor—so keep conversations, recommendations, and loans relatable to the client's issues.

Philosophy

Philosophy is concerned with the nature of existence, truth, and reality. These are very broad concepts, and they can be overwhelming. The point of studying philosophy is not to simply become more academic and well-read. It is to compare, contrast, and explore different concepts so you can develop your own. Being able to share or cite historical thinkers' perceptions when they're relevant not only makes a good impression, but it can be very helpful. No single philosophy is an absolute, comprehensive truth, but by borrowing and honoring many of them, you have tremendous access to perceptions, concepts, and ideas that may be catalysts to a client.

In addition, having general knowledge of philosophical concepts affixes those concepts in your subconscious, adding layers to your own thinking. It is not necessary to quote a particular philosopher. Trust that you're building a subtle database of philosophical ideas. Over time, you will intuitively be able to draw on those concepts when they're applicable.

I briefly had a mentor in my hypnotherapy training who quoted prolifically. He was able to quote actual sayings and phrases from many great thinkers, scientists, authors, comedians, and politicians. While I was impressed by his ability to retain these quotes, it was the actual concepts that were valuable to me. I myself could not retain the quotes, but their meaning and the influence they had on my thoughts were helpful.

Do not strive to memorize actual quotes; instead, process the concepts and ideas that are valuable to you. It makes little difference how many sentences you can quote if you don't know their meaning, and there's no value in quoting an idea word for word if you can't communicate the meaning or lesson attached to it.

Student Exercise

Below is a list of philosophers. Review the names and their general concepts online to see which ones you want to know more about. As you peruse their names, other names will emerge; like a domino effect, one thing leads to another.

- Sartre
- Kierkegaard
- Marx

- Plato
- Socrates
- Pythagoras (who coined the term *philosophy*)
- Lao Tzu

I encourage you to discover the philosophical principles each of these thinkers had and to look into other philosophies too. Not only is it unnecessary to memorize quotes, but it isn't even necessary to memorize their principles. If the most you retain is the concepts, you've retained the most important part. Remember that the best way to retain information is to become familiar, not to memorize or study.

Religion and Spirituality

You should also know the basics of the five major religions, including what each designates as a goal (e.g., heaven or enlightenment), the basic teachings, key players, and major historical events. Each major religion (listed below) has multiple offshoots, and each has a mystical sect as well (listed in parentheses). I meet many people who are confessed adherents to a specific religion, yet they know nearly nothing of its actual dogma or key figures. Review the list below of the world's major religions. You should be able to answer the following questions in general terms: Who are the main personalities (whom is it centered around)? In what time period did it begin, and what is its relationship to other religions? Is there a head leader?

Major World Religions

- Christianity (Rosicrucianism)
- Judaism (kabbalah)
- Islam (Sufism)
- Hinduism (Yog, Gyan, Karm, Bhakt)
- Buddhism (technically a mystical tradition, not a spiritual philosophy)

When you review these, you will find beautiful things in all of them. Eventually you can develop the ability to refer to a particular component that you respect, admire, or find value in. For example, while I am not Muslim, I find the concept of the *fitrah* wise and useful (the concept that we all have a true sense of wrong and right and that ignorance of written law is no excuse). Muslims feel that a person has a moral compass within and knows, innately, that stealing is wrong, regardless of whether such is taught.

I'm a follower of Eastern philosophy and religion. Eastern religions are often considered liberal and open systems, whereas Western ones are considered closed, or sectarian. A so-called open system allows the inclusion of other concepts as long as the ultimate goal is identified and the other concepts can assist in reaching that goal. On the other hand a closed system instructs that involvement with another system neutralizes and harms the system and the individual.

I had a client who was a devout Mormon. Mormonism is popularly perceived as a right-wing religion and is considered "closed." Some of the best spiritual conversations I ever had were when he and I talked about our love for God, our devotion to the divine, and our struggles to evolve spiritually. His closed religion advises him not to associate with anyone regarding spiritual matters other than those of the same faith. Yet we bonded over our gratitude and love for the divine, and our religious differences were never an issue. Both of us learned a lot.

I can hold my own when discussing (or even debating) Western religious concepts even though I practice Eastern religions. I often know much more about those religions than those who actually belong to them. In general, this forges respect; on only two occasions did being from a less conventional religion prove to be an issue. During counseling sessions, focus should not be on your own particular belief system but on the general concepts. It makes little difference if you believe in the same religious rules as your clients. Your role is to help them adhere to what *they* believe in. This Mormon man I worked with would occasionally indulge in beer and wine despite his religion's opposition to such, and he was conflicted with guilt. While I personally felt his relationship with alcohol was harmless, I helped him achieve his goal, which was to adhere to the letter of his religious beliefs.

Below are some recommended topics and materials on religion and spirituality:

Western Spirituality/Philosophy

- *Jesus Calling* (Young)
- *St. Francis of Assisi: A Biography* (Englebert)
- *The Complete Idiot's Guide to the Bible*

Eastern Spirituality/Philosophy

- *Autobiography of a Yogi* (Yogananda)
- *Be Here Now* (Ram Das)
- *Bhagavad Gita* (various authors [with commentary by Swami Mukundanand is the one I recommend])
- *Caitanya Caratamrit* (Krishn Dasa Kaviraja)
- Any books about or by Rupa Goswami, Jiva Goswami, or Sanatana Goswami
- The *I Ching*
- *The Buddha* (a PBS documentary) and various biographical accounts

Science

I recommend a few main topics:

- Physics: Look into the general theory of relativity, the special theory of relativity, and string theory.
- Biology: Learn the fundamentals. I bought a picture book from Amazon that gives amazing details of bones, tissues, organs, and systems.

180

- Zoology: Most people are into animals, especially pets, so this can be a great rapport builder.
- Geology: Learn some basics on how the Earth works and when it formed, the oceans, skies, and so on.
- Astronomy: How old is the universe? The planet? What is *accretion*?
- Chemistry: Know the difference between an atom and molecule and the basic elements.

Once again, there is no need to be an expert; in fact, the opportunity to cite scientific facts may never even come up. But having a general understanding of the material phenomena we exist in expands your understanding of how things work, how they fit together, and why. As you learn basic scientific knowledge, you may find yourself using examples to emphasize, make points, and clarify concepts through metaphor and analogy. Some recommended reading and topics are listed below:

- *The Elegant Universe* (Greene)
- *The Theory of Everything* (Hawking)
- *A Brief History of Time* (Hawking)
- *The Ape That Spoke* (McCrone)

Metaphysics

Metaphysics is a wide area, and it makes no difference if you "believe" in metaphysics or not. These are widely accepted concepts, and it is best to be familiar with them.

Recommended reading and topics are below:

Alternative Thinking

- *The Powers of Thought* (Aivanhov)
- *The Secret Doctrine* (Blavatsky)
- *Wheels of Life: A User's Guide to the Chakra System* (Anodea Judith)
- *Sorcerer's Stone: A Beginners Guide to Alchemy* (Hauck)

- *The Complete Idiot's Guide to Alchemy* (Hauck)
- astrology
- psychic phenomena (clairvoyance, ESP)
- fate

I can't say enough about the *Complete Idiot's Guide* series. They are typically well produced, thorough, and accurate. You can be an idiot to read one, but you won't be one when you're done! They are great primers on any subject.

So many books stand out to me and have contributed to my worldview and character. I cannot say they will have the same effect on anyone else. These recommendations cover a wide spectrum, so I want to emphasize that the wider your wisdom and knowledge are, the more they will enrich you and make you an enriching person, too. The more you know and are aware of, the better version of yourself you are and the more you'll have to offer the world you live in. Dabble, sample, and experiment. You may like a few selections I recommend, hate a few, and love a few. Or you'll love or hate them all—it's up to you!

16

COUNSELING MODALITIES

By studying and reviewing different counseling modalities, you will have access to as many ways as possible to help people and communicate with them.

You do not have to practice or adhere to any specific modality or science, but you should be informed about what the population has access to and the ones you may be able to use as well. It is best to borrow from several modalities and synthesize parts of them to create the best possible strategy to assist an individual.

This book is designed to teach you how to begin and sustain a private practice. All of the practical and technical issues that need to be addressed to establish a private practice are here. This book is not designed to teach you how to be a counselor. Your combined training, education, and life experience is the school for being a good counselor.

If you follow all of the instructions within this book, you will be able to establish and sustain a private practice, as long as you contribute the final, most essential, ingredient: being good at counseling.

Without good counseling, it makes no difference how much training and education you receive or how great your office, website, or wardrobe is. If you do not get results and know how to be a good counselor, your practice will fail. I would love to tell you that anyone with enough passion, resources, and training can be a good counselor, but I do not believe this to be true. Some innate, instinctual talent is needed to succeed at this job. Some professions extend beyond technical skill and training and require raw, innate talent. Consider opera singing: give me all the voice lessons you want with the best vocal coach on the planet, and teach me all of the arias known to man—I still can't sing!

Becoming a good counselor takes time. Your instincts and skills must develop. Experience is needed, and experience can only be acquired by doing, not through academic, learning.

Passion, desire, confidence, self-awareness, imagination, and vision *combined* with education and academic knowledge and time in the trenches will sustain your practice. Nothing less.

This section will give you fundamental insights and approaches for counseling and suggest modalities for you to study and experiment with. No matter what modalities are mentioned and reviewed, there are always more. I present some of what I feel has been beneficial to my practice's success and have included some of my own. After more than ten years of counseling (over twenty thousand hours) I have morphed and fused so many concepts and modalities that it is difficult to know anymore where my own invented methods begin and those I've used end.

In this section, we will do a brief, fundamental review of Freud, Jung, Rollnick, Kappas, myself and others. These reviews can be used as a starting point; whichever modalities seem valuable and attract your attention should be explored further. Explore them further online, and if your interest waxes even more, you can consider investing in a book for more thorough study. Over time, you should have access to several modalities and be able to fuse them. While an artist may have his own favorite color, he uses the entire spectrum of colors and brushstrokes to create an image. We do not need to marry a specific modality and use nothing else. We may learn many and never find them relevant or useful at all, but we may discover one that is particularly useful and resonates with our own approach.

It is better to know and discard a modality than to need one and not know of it.

Motivational Interviewing

Motivational Interviewing (MI) is a counseling modality that was first described in 1983 by William R. Miller, PhD. It was developed by 1991 with Stephen Rollnick, PhD. The concept of MI is to assist clients in reaching sensible conclusions that will motivate and inspire them to follow through with behavioral changes.

The counselor's role in MI is to lead the client toward sensible and effective conclusions for healthy change by asking questions that inevitably lead to these conclusions. Because clients perceive these conclusions as their own, they are personally motivated to act on them. Simply being told what is the right and sensible course of action is remote and impersonal and is typically met with some resistance from the subconscious. But a conclusion personally arrived at comes with a sense of ownership, and ownership creates powerful motivation and commitment.

It is said, "You can lead a horse to water, but you can't make him drink." Maybe not, but you can lead a horse to water and make the water so appealing that it is hard to resist! The horse (client) is already thirsty (wanting to change and improve), and if he is given access to a cool, bucolic stream that is refreshing and tasty, it is almost certain he will drink.

Lead your clients to conclusions. Ask questions and interview them to bring them to the right answers. Below is a sample dialogue with a client who has decided to exercise more frequently.

"So you're thinking of working out more. That's good. How often?"

"You know...a couple times a week would be good."

"Oh, so, like, twice per week?"

"Yep."

"Which days?"

"The days I get off early and don't feel drained from work would be best. Most days I feel drained, but a couple times a week I usually feel pretty good."

"Is it hard to know in advance which days you'll feel good and which days you'll feel drained?"

"Yeah, I can't know until the end of the day, usually."

"Here's my concern: if we don't determine things like days and times in advance, we may just say, 'Well, tomorrow will work,' and next thing we know, a week has gone by with no exercise. Isn't that how you became less active in the first place?"

"Yeah...kinda."

"I bet sometimes you wake up to go to work and don't feel like going, yet you do. You don't get to set the work schedule, and your employer has no access to how you feel about working that day, nor does he care. Similarly, if your workout schedule was set and inflexible and you had obvious consequences if you missed it, you'd probably override the lack of motivation and follow it, too. Kinda like work: we would much prefer to be independently wealthy. If we were, even if we liked our work, we would be more selective on our commitment. At the end of the year, if we didn't have to or need to work, we'd probably skip more often!"

"No doubt."

"So, what would happen if you set a fitness schedule and made it firm—not reliant upon how you feel?"

"I guess it'd help, but I'd still know I had a choice, so..."

"Yeah, but you've got a choice with work, too. It's not illegal to stay home, skip work, and let it all go. You could go live in a cave and forget the rat race! Technically, it's a choice to work and pay bills. We both know there're people who choose not to. Your decision to work is self-imposed. Even obeying the law is a choice and self-imposed. There are a lot of people in prison who chose not to obey. Right?"

"True. Lots."

"Are we more likely to work out if we force ourselves? Or just consciously make a self-imposed rule about it, the way we do with our jobs and other responsibilities?"

"Uh…force?"

"You seem unsure of your answer, but let's look at it. You've been trying to force yourself to exercise for months now. How's that working?"

"Not so good. That's why I'm here looking for help."

"That's what I thought. And yet you go to work, and you came here, too. The whole reason we set an appointment is because it creates a sense of obligation within our minds. We don't do squat if we don't feel obligated. I mean, other than things that give us pleasure. But work and things like dental appointments—we keep those commitments because we feel obligated once we make the arrangements. If you decide to work out on three specific days per week, identify and designate those days, and set them firm in your mind, would you feel more obligated and likely follow through?"

"Yeah, I keep my commitments, once they're made. It bugs me when other people don't, so I do."

"Sounds like you found your own solution. Designate your workout days, and set them in stone in your mind. Pick specific days and times in advance. Start with something reasonable, and work your way up as it becomes more habitual. If you pick Mondays and Thursdays, then you keep 'em. Unless there is a nuclear holocaust or the zombie apocalypse, you keep 'em. In other words, when real obligations or emergencies arise, you modify and adapt, but being tired does not qualify. Right?"

"That seems reasonable. I can do that. I'll try."

"Try it for the first two weeks, and when we meet again, we'll review how it went and how it felt. And if there's anything wrong with the system, we'll modify it or scrap it! Until we see if it works or not—and why—we have nothing to modify."

The shorter, less effective version of this would have been to simply instruct the client. Engaging him in the process and leading him to the conclusion makes his decision feel personal, which means it will be accepted consciously and even subconsciously. The short version is quicker and less involved, but it does not motivate by facilitating a sense of ownership of the results.

The plan also has a built-in need for review, establishing good reason to meet again and creating opportunity for further sessions and work. As the saying goes, Rome wasn't built in a day. It is not reasonable to expect to resolve an issue in a single session. While it is not ethical to deliberately create topics and issues to encourage gratuitous sessions, future sessions are often necessary for follow-up and follow-through.

If you keep the MI philosophy in mind (leading clients to the sensible conclusion), opportunities to apply it will reveal themselves.

I've been applying MI for years; in fact, I had been using it long before I was formally introduced to it. When I shared some of my methods with a colleague, he quickly identified them as MI and gave me Rollnick's book to read. I was pleased that there was a formal teaching of these methods. I often use a parallel-universe or time-

188

travel paradigm: I ask a client to pretend we've traveled into the future or to a parallel universe where he has already accomplished his goals. Then I ask him to consider how his success with this goal changed his life in this alternate universe. A thorough examination of the ultimate goal is extrapolated until actual, intimate reasoning is established between the client and his or her motivation.

Freudian Psychology (Sigmund Freud 1856–1939)

Freud is the pioneer and founder of psychoanalysis, and psychoanalysis is the bedrock of all modalities. By dividing the mind into the conscious and unconscious, Freud founded the theory that our unconscious mind is responsible for our conscious behaviors. Conscious decisions, he claimed, are subordinate to, regulated by, and decided upon by the unconscious, which is below our level of awareness. The unconscious uses a model to form all of its decisions, and this model, Freud said, is formed by all of our life experiences: that is, we are the sum total of all of our prior events and perceptions. This means that if a child is bit by a dog when the mind is forming its model of the world, the unconscious will categorize dogs as a source of pain and fear, regulating and influencing future perceptions of them. Likewise, if a child has a positive experience on a roller-coaster ride, the unconscious will categorize roller coasters as fun and positive. If a feature of that positive roller-coaster experience was being validated and accepted through bonding with a parent, roller coasters will also be associated with the bonding experience, even though they are not technically the source. Events are thus linked by association.

Id, Ego, and Superego

The id stage, as Freud explained it, is associated with infancy, the stage of life when we are driven by our basic needs (food, shelter, love, and affection) and trying to acquire them.

The ego develops as a child begins to interact with the world and establishes relationships: mother, father, brother, dog, and the spectrum of actions and reactions. During the ego stage, the child's model of the world is developing and becoming more complex.

The superego is the mature state, when the mind can and does continue to expand well beyond itself and fundamental relationships. The superego develops conceptually; that is, it is capable of defining and forming values and principles.

Below is a summary of Freudian psychology.

1. Character and personality are determined by events in early childhood.
2. Attitude and perception are influenced by irrational drives from the unconscious, *irrational* meaning they do not appear to be rational to conscious awareness.
3. Defense mechanisms form within the mind to protect these attitudes and perceptions by resisting the conscious will to change them.
4. Mental or emotional disturbances are expressions of these defense mechanisms, which try to protect our model of the world. The conflicts between the conscious and unconscious manifest in varying expressions and to various degrees (e.g., neurosis, anxiety, depression, and so on).
5. Through conscious awareness of these expressions and their origins, liberation from them occurs.

Freud's theory is based on the assumption that learning the genesis of a behavior brings full awareness of the behavior. Liberation from the behavior occurs when full awareness of it is realized.

This can, and does, happen in many instances. Unfortunately, there are also occasions when the genesis of a behavior is brought into conscious awareness and the individual is retraumatized instead. I've seen it.

Sometimes psychoanalysis offers perspective and understanding but not liberation. Sometimes the issue stays the same, sometimes it gets better, and sometimes it gets worse.

Jungian Psychology (Carl Jung 1875–1961)

Carl Gustav Jung was a protégé of Freud. He expanded Freudian psychology to include philosophy, literature, mysticism, alchemy, astrology and both Eastern and Western religions and spirituality,.

Jung stood on the shoulders of Freud to establish and pioneer his own concepts by expanding Freudian theories and evolving them. It is doubtful that Jungian psychology would exist if it wasn't for Freud. Eventually the two men became somewhat adversarial. Freud, the teacher, felt threatened by Jung, the student. Jung himself became a master, and many feel he surpassed Freud.

Jung conceived of the "collective unconscious," the concept that there is a network of ideas, values, and beliefs that societies and cultures have in common based on the majority of people believing and thinking similarly. Members of the society, Jung believed, are not required to be officially taught a concept or value in order to adopt it. By sheer magnitude, the frequency of a value is unconsciously received and adopted. (If you're interested, search "one hundredth monkey effect" online).

Jung also introduced the concept of the "archetype," an original model or ideal that expresses a concept. Jung proposed we are all influenced by certain symbols, sounds, and other stimuli because they are archetypal: they exist in our unconscious and have fixed, universal meanings that stimulate associations. The origin of an archetype does not exist; it is such an original concept that

191

it exists independently of origin. Take, for instance, a square. The shape of a square was not invented; it has always existed, and everyone has a similar sense of it. It represents foundation and stability, and this is the impression everyone, everywhere, has of it. The meaning of any archetype is innate and aboriginal.

Milton Erickson (1902–1994)

Milton Erickson established hypnosis as a powerful and useful modality in psychology. He had an inexplicable talent that even he himself could not quite nail down or explain. His hypnosis techniques were intuitive, and he was mostly self-taught. His work inspired neurolinguistic programming (NLP) and many professionals. My own style, counterintuitive counseling, was influenced by Erickson as well.

Erickson was unconventional, as he often used himself and personal stories to illustrate his ideas. In general, the therapeutic community is reminded not to divulge personal opinions or emotions and to maintain a quality of remoteness in interaction in order to maintain objectivity for the counselor and the client. However, I have had tremendous success in using personal examples of relevant situations. When I speak from my own perspective, clients respond; the instructions given have clout, as they transcend theoretical. It is important to note that using yourself as a personal example should only be done when it is relevant. Counselors should not go gratuitously into detail about their personal lives. Small amounts to break the ice in a session are appropriate, but you must be careful not to dominate the session with personal issues or stories. Every few minutes, the conversation should always be shifted back to the client.

Erickson had an uncanny ability to hypnotize people without formal induction. His mastery of behavioral driving mechanisms is worth looking into further. He once put a man in a hypnotic trance by merely shaking the man's hand. Within moments, the man seemed oblivious

192

to Erickson's shaking his hand. While Erickson shook his hand and spoke to him, the man went into a trance, and Erickson made a hypnotic suggestion that broke him of the toxic behavior he had. When Erickson was asked how he had done it, he said he didn't know. He said it was spontaneous and intuitive: he went with his instincts, and the man was healed.

John Kappas (1925–2002)

John Kappas is the founder of the Hypnosis Motivation Institute (HMI), in California. Kappas stood on the herculean shoulders of Milton Erickson. Kappas was also a pioneer, developing Ericksonian techniques and helping form them into applicable modalities. Kappas and his E&P theory have been discussed in detail in the section on hypnotherapy.

Cognitive Behavioral Therapy

Cognitive behavioral therapy (CBT) is not applied for general improvement, but is focused on specific issues or problems. It is a process of analysis and action. Through analysis, the client gains insight into a problem or behavior to understand how it works and what circumstances or conditions trigger it. The action component is the application of specific strategies to the behavior or problem to neutralize or eliminate it.

Any strategy that alters perception and behavior qualifies as CBT (e.g., dieting, exercising, abstinence), and any new behavior that is a better alternative to an existing one is CBT.

CBT is something of a catchall modality, but significant emphasis should be placed on the behavioral aspect of it. Clients will not be satisfied with realizations, regardless of how profound they are. All realizations should have actionable strategies applied to them.

193

I recommend a gradated approach (G-CBT)—behavior modification in stages or steps.[15] Let's use the example of weight loss and fitness:

Using a purely cognitive approach, the counselor would say, "If you lose weight and get fit, you will feel better and be healthier."

Using a purely behavioral approach, the counselor would say, "Eat less, and work out more."

CBT, on the other hand, would entail pairing the concept of feeling better and healthier with an actual strategy of working out and eating less. How better would the client feel, and in what ways? The answer to that question is the cognitive aspect. Then the counselor would design a healthy diet and fitness routine—the behavioral aspect: "You should work out five days a week, eat only healthy foods that are low in carbs and high in protein, skip dessert, and don't eat after seven o'clock at night."

My approach, G-CBT, would (1) acknowledge the current lifestyle behavior, (2) establish what the ideal diet and fitness routine would be, (3) compare the ideal routine and the current one, and (4) design a progressive, step-by-step strategy, bridging the actual to the ideal. What follows is a detailed mathematical formula for this process, provided simply as example. The concept is what is important here. The formula can be adapted to any behavior once the concept is understood.

> You currently have a 4,000-calorie diet with random desserts and little awareness of portion size or frequency of eating, and you exercise three times per week for twenty minutes—all weights, no cardio. Your ideal diet would be a 2,300-calorie diet, moderate and infrequent desserts and indulgences, and a sixty-minute workout, including cardio, four times per week.

---

[15] G-CBT: gradated cognitive behavioral treatment—my own qualification.

Let's allow three months (twelve weeks) to progress from the current routine to the ideal routine. Let's subtract the lower numbers from the higher ones to establish needed modifications:

Calories: 4,000 calories (current) – 2,000 calories (ideal) = 2000 ÷ 12 weeks = 166 calories.

This figure means that you should reduce calorie intake by approximately 166 each week until the ideal number is reached. The gradated process minimizes subconscious resistance by not creating a state of deprivation (the 166-calorie adjustment will be barely noticed at all). By the time the ideal quantity is achieved, the new behavior is habitual: the subconscious, which is in charge of sustaining habits and behaviors, has adapted.

Now let's look at the fitness routine. Four hours each week is the ideal, and one hour is the current routine.

4 (ideal) – 1 (current) = 3

3 ÷ 12 (weeks) = .25 (¼ hour)

If we divide the quarter of an hour by the number of ideal workout days (four), we get approximately five minutes added onto each twenty-minute workout period. If you increase the current workout time by five minutes each week for twelve weeks, it will gradually increase to the ideal one-hour workout time. Add one workout day to the first three weeks (three times per week) and then another in week four (four times per week).

Over a twelve-week span, you will have adjusted the diet and the workout to ideal amounts, and the results will be observable. Ideal fitness and weight is inevitable as long as the new routines are sustained.

It takes approximately ninety days—twelve weeks—to create a habit within the mind. Anything shorter can be overrun by existing conditioned behaviors and habits. Once new habits are established and are sustained for an additional ninety days, they become habitual. All habits are created this way—by repetition and association—and become firm after approximately ninety days of consistent repetition. The subconscious does not know the difference between good and bad. These are conscious concepts that are irrelevant and abstract to the subconscious. The subconscious will enforce, reinforce, and protect any behavior it is conditioned to.

Note that the G-CBT process breaks the bond the subconscious has with a behavior. Once the bond is broken, a new habit or behavior can be installed through the same process all behaviors and habits are installed by: repetition (completing an action over and over again) and association (consciously and consistently defining the behavior as good or healthy).

The client and counselor can modify and refine the process over the course of the modification as any faults or defects in the strategy reveal themselves. If the client increases workout time by five minutes but consistently only achieves three of those five, the time can be modified to four minutes. If the client consistently achieves five minutes without struggle or effort, the length can be increased to six. Any increase or decrease should be moderate, not aggressive.

Exposure-Response Therapy

Exposure-response therapy (ERP) is a system of exposing the client to a fear or phobia in minimal to moderate amounts and gradually increasing the amount in order to achieve desensitization to the fear or phobia response. This method is often used in the treatment of obsessive compulsive disorder (OCD), post traumatic stress disorder (PTSD), and phobias.

ERP Case Conference

A client had developed post PTSD from a car accident, making her afraid to drive. At first she could not bring herself to go through the specific intersection near her home where the accident had occurred. Within a few weeks, she could not go down any street that even led to the intersection. Within a few months, she could not leave her driveway without having symptoms of a panic attack.

We combined G-CBT with exposure-response therapy.

1. Each day for one week, she held her car keys in her hand while she watched TV, made dinner, or completed other duties. This desensitized her to their presence.
2. Each day for one week, she went into the garage (without her keys) to sit for seven minutes inside the car. This desensitized her to the car atmosphere/stimuli.
   a. While sitting in the car, she performed breathing and calming exercises she'd learned in our session. These exercises were done to bring her fear down in magnitude: her anxiety level of six was brought to four over the seven minutes. If she could not bring it to a four within seven minutes, the exercise was postponed to avoid retraumatizing the client.
   b. The same calming exercises were performed in our office sessions, using visualizations accompanied by calming hypnotic suggestions.
3. Each day for the first week, she performed the breathing and calming exercises in the car, but now with her keys in her hand or on the dash or console, where she could see them.
4. For three consecutive days, she put the key in the ignition and started the car. She then shut the car off immediately.
   a. The following four days, she started the ignition and allowed

        the car to idle in a stationary
        position.

  b. While the car was running and
       idle, she performed her calming
       exercises.

5. Every day in week five, she coasted the car into the driveway and back to the garage.

6. During week six she drove out of the driveway and onto the street in front of the house, parked, and then returned to the driveway.

7. In week seven she drove to the corner and back—that's it.

8. In the eighth week, she drove around the block.

By week eight she was getting a bit bored with the exercises; they were becoming routine. That was an indication of healing. This progression went on for several more weeks, with the trips becoming increasingly longer—to the local store, a nearby friend's house, and so on. In week eleven, she arrived for her appointment with me as scheduled. She greeted me with a laugh and tossed her keys at me! She had driven—over six miles on the freeway—to come to her appointment. Mission accomplished! When we discontinued our work together after a total of thirteen weeks, she was driving everywhere she needed to with low but manageable levels of anxiety or fear.

Evidence-Based Treatment

Evidence-based treatment (EBT) is not a specific modality. It is any form of treatment that can be verified through research and that the therapeutic community has collectively accepted. If this definition seems vague, that's because it is. All of the aforementioned modalities can be considered evidence based, as they are accepted and documented in the helping community as being effective. The modalities and approaches reviewed here are just a few. The included modalities are prevalent and established in the helping community.

Recommended Reading

I fully acknowledge that there are volumes of material I've never been exposed to that would benefit me. My exposure is limited to the circumstances and events of my life (as are yours). These recommendations are just a gesture:

Psychology

- *E&P: Relationship Strategies* (Kappas)
- *Motivational Interviewing* (Miller & Rollnick)
- Freudian psychology (many books that introduce and give basics)
- Jung (many books that introduce and give basics)
- Cognitive Behavioral Therapy (CBT)
- *DSM-V*
- *Yes, Your Teen Is Crazy* (Bradley)
- *Tormenting Thoughts and Secret Rituals* (Osborne)
- *Sleep: The Mysteries, the Problems, and the Solutions* (Schenck)
- *Patterns of the Hypnotic Techniques of Milton Erikson* (Bandler & Grinder)

Addiction

- *In the Realm of Hungry Ghosts* (Mate)
- *Project Addiction: The Complete Guide to Using, Abusing, and Recovering from Drugs and Behaviors* (Spackey)
- *Alive Again* (Samuels)

17

APPEARANCE

Our role in clients' lives is very personal. We are expecting strangers to expose their inner thoughts, feelings, fears, and bad behaviors to us. We want them to see us as a friend and ally, and yet we are not friends: we are their counselors, and they are our clients. Though I feel friendly toward every one of my clients, we cannot go to the movies or to dinner or have our sessions over lunch. Any interaction outside of the office changes the relationship to a dual one and is therefore inappropriate, unethical, and counterproductive.

The role of mentor and counselor must be constant. When you come to a client's mind, he or she should think of you in this context. Your appearance can either help sustain or detract from this.

It is unlikely that anyone will complain if you wear jeans and a T-shirt during sessions, but doing so takes you subtly out of context. A photograph on your desk may show you in beach attire with the kids, but in the office you must dress as a professional. Businesspeople wear business attire, athletes wear team uniforms, and counselors should wear attire that is professional and yet casual. You're not a stockbroker, so leave the executive wear in the closet. You're not at the beach, either, so put on some shoes—not sandals, but shoes! And no shorts!

Your role as an authority in clients' lives must be consistent. While it is OK to modify and improve your appearance over time, these shifts should be subtle and not drastic.

Dress well and dress appropriately.

Men

Men should wear slacks, comfortable, casual shoes with matching socks (yes, shoes and socks should be in same color spectrum!). Your belt should match your shoes (not your tie—your shoes). Most shirts should be tucked in. If not tucked in, a shirt should extend past the belt buckle and about midway through the crotch area, but not past it. Clothes should fit your body—nothing tight or too loose, and never baggy.

Your office attire should be different from your casual attire. If you like polo shirts and Dockers at home or slacks and button-down shirts in everyday life, it can be tempting to use the same wardrobe in the office, as these are technically appropriate. However, your subconscious needs to transition to the counselor role, and a change of clothes helps that occur. Purchasing a set of polo shirts and button-downs exclusively for the office is a fine way to accommodate. Changing your clothes when you go to the office will help you to shift mentally into the role of counselor. Likewise, when you leave the office and change into casual clothes at home, you transition from counselor to mom, dad, spouse, or neighbor.

Women

Women should wear slacks and comfortable, casual dress shoes with matching socks or nylons. Accessories can be used to subtly enhance appearance, but they should not be worn to gain attention. Jewelry should follow the same rule: it should be an attractive enhancement, not loud, garish, or distracting. Skirts should come to or below the knee and worn with blouses that are comfortable and refined. Dresses are also appropriate, but they also should not be distracting, awkward, or uncomfortable to wear. Clothes should fit your body; nothing should be tight or too loose.

Comfort is important. It makes no difference how great you look if you are constantly squirming or shifting in your seat to adjust your body to be at ease. Counseling is a sit-down job, so you will need clothes that allow you to sit comfortably for long hours and do not wrinkle much by the end of the day.

Unless you have an uncle in the dry-cleaning business, you will want clothes that wear well. To control dry-cleaning costs, I typically wear the same outfit for the entire week. I see most clients weekly, so they don't see me in the same outfit in consecutive sessions. The clothes are comfortable and don't wrinkle much. A quick ironing midweek keeps me from looking disheveled for the rest of the week. By using one set of clothes per week, I do not have to keep track of what I've worn the day before or in the last session I had with a particular client. Once one set is worn for a week, it goes into my dry-clean pile. Once I've gone through my entire set of four to seven outfits, I drop them off at the cleaners. This system assures me that my clients only see me in the same outfit every forth to eighth session and lowers dry-cleaning costs and the chore of dropping the clothes off.

I own two pairs of black shoes and two pairs of brown shoes, which I alternate. I switch from dark to brown attire every two to three weeks and wear the appropriate shoes. I invest in one or two new shirts, ties, and pairs of slacks each year so my wardrobe stays fresh and fashionable without the cost of an entire wardrobe every year. About every other year, I donate one or two outfits to a charity. This pace of purchasing and donating keeps my wardrobe rotating. Fresh and current is important.

I recommend getting fashion advice: Ask a friend of the opposite sex what he or she thinks of your clothes when you buy them. Do not ask salespeople: their job is to sell, which influences their judgment. Do not ask people of same sex. Same-sex friends do not see you in the context of attractive versus unattractive. We want to be harmlessly attractive. Famous actor Tom Hanks once said in an interview that part of his success was attributed to the fact people found him neither attractive nor unattractive.

Women found him moderately attractive, but not distractingly so, and men did not find him threatening.

If you're hot, play it down. If you're not, play it up!

Hair

Men should have well-trimmed hair and keep it consistent; this usually means a cut every three to four weeks. It makes no difference if you have medium-length hair, long hair, or a crew cut. What matters is that the cut you have is clean. You can have a beard and hair past your ears if you look good and like it, but be sure the overall look and cut appears deliberate, not like a just-got-out-of-bed mistake.

Women may have long or short hair; either is all right, but it, too, should look deliberate. Find the look that's right for you personally, and stick with it, or at least very similar versions of it.

Fitness

To be a responsible mentor you must walk the walk. You do not need to be perfectly fit, trim, and in shape, but you need to practice what you preach, and what we're preaching as counselors is how to live in a responsible, reasonable way while maintaining and honoring our uniqueness. Work out and follow a sensible diet. It's OK to have your indulgences; struggling to stay fit is common. My being less than perfectly fit and trim (far less!) allows me to bond with clients, yet I can speak from example on how to try and keep trying even when you are not getting the results you wish for. I may not be my ideal weight, but I'd be so much worse off if I didn't have discipline and routine.

Establish a moderately healthy diet and a regular fitness routine, two times a week minimally. You will feel and be healthier and be able to advise and relate to clients while living the lifestyle you are advocating. It is essential to practice what you preach. Most people would not choose a fitness trainer who is clearly out of shape, a dentist with bad teeth, or a hairdresser with a bad hairdo! Likewise, they won't choose a counselor who is unstable. If we are not organized or intelligent enough to package ourselves presentably, why would anyone trust our advice? Very few people can perform so perfectly that an unkempt appearance is ignored. Einstein got away with it, but he's Albert Einstein—the icon of intellect!

A Book by Its Cover

Your appearance and lifestyle are an actual part of your practice, the same as your furniture and office. They are tools of your trade. Your defects and faults are raw materials that can be used to bond with clients, and your successes are examples as well. We must ask clients to do as we do, not just as we say. In many occupations and careers, appearance and impressions can be insignificant, but as counselors we fulfill a role of inspiring and motivating others to the best they can be—not the best overall, but the best they can be.

This is not to imply that establishing a practice requires a perfect appearance. Clients seek you to help them mature, evolve, and grow into their ideals. We are all a work in progress, so be steady with your work so that clients will be inspired by you to do the same, regardless of the gap between what you're trying for and what you actually are.

18
OFFICE

A professional appearance is required of a counselor, and your place of practice is an extension of who you are. It can be tempting to begin in a storage space, garage, or spare room in your home or apartment. While these choices are frugal, the majority of clients will categorize you as someone not to be taken seriously. In a perfect world, we would all evaluate others—and be evaluated—by skill and expertise alone and not by outer appearances, but we do not live in a perfect world.

It can be tempting to take out loans and use credit cards to secure a premium office, furniture, an expensive wardrobe, and the executive-style BMW to impress the community. However, there is no need for or value in leveraging your resources to the point of anxiety and stress. Too much anxiety and stress will compromise your ability to serve your clients with clarity.

Look on Craigslist to find inexpensive office space, and consider subletting. If you do not see a suitable space offered, place a want ad yourself. It is unnecessary to have a full-time office in the beginning. By subletting space, you can share expenses while still having a professional environment. There are typically lots of therapists, counselors, real-estate agents, accountants, and other professionals that are looking for subletters.

A sublet office space should be somewhat reflective of your profession. A medical environment with an exam bed is uncomfortable, and an office decorated in Harley Davidson and comic-book memorabilia is awkward.

My first sublet office was with a real-estate executive: with a desk, a couple of plants, and some generic wall hangings—it was functional. I was able to keep a small box of my photos and documents in a corner, and when I arrived, I would remove the real-estate executive's family photos and replace them with mine, also taking down her license and replacing it with my own certifications. Upon leaving I would remove my belongings and replace her photos and documents. It was easy and quick to transform her office into my office and back again. I had a private office without the burden of the cost interfering with my work and my focus.

I've had plenty of clients share details about professionals they sought out or tried before calling me. Many of them had offices in their home or garage, and my clients said this was a real turnoff.

We cannot think too small. But we cannot think too big, either.

It is tempting to take out a loan and secure the best space, but this is premature. Many start-ups fail because they leverage resources before their practice is established. Grow proportionately.

My first office was in a very nice executive building. Down the hall from me was a hypnotherapist who had gone to the same school I attended and had started six months earlier than I. I walked by her office daily to get to my sublet space. I couldn't help but see her grand mahogany desk and leather reclining chair for clients. Her space was impressive. She had a wall full of documents, and she dressed sharply. I was intimidated. We were office neighbors for eight months, until I moved on to my own office.

Five years later she contacted me: she was broke. She had borrowed money from her bank to pay for marketing, to rent the office, and acquire more and more training. Now she was asking me if I would sublet my space to her. She was practicing from her garage at home, and it wasn't going well. I had to decline because my practice was so strong by that time that I had sessions from nine in the morning until seven in the evening, as well as half days on Saturdays and Sundays.

I don't know where she is today. I hope she made it, but I suspect she did not. I do not see any sign of her practice in the community I live in.

Pace yourself. If you're in this for the long haul, the nice office will happen.

Be in it for the long haul: don't overreach.

Right Space, Right Time

I enjoy my current office.[16] It has plenty of windows that overlook the park across the street, and it is spacious enough that I do not feel claustrophobic by midday. Clients, too, are subconsciously set at ease because they do not need to spend even one brain cell adapting to an awkward, unsightly, or uncomfortable space. They can come in, sit down, and be at ease. In addition, a comfortable office makes a subtle subconscious impression: it implies success.

A nice office shows clients that you are good enough at what you do to sustain rent on a good location. Minimalist décor expresses simplicity, yet a small amount of style and some personal features (family photos, a few cool paintings on the walls) can express small amounts about you. These should not dominate the room, however. The theme of the room should be one of practical comfort that is conventional (sofa, table, desk, and so on) yet unique. Convention is needed, as every client has different tastes, and it is useful to blend in. But lack of convention is needed too in order to express uniqueness and creative

---

[16] There are photos and a video tour of my office on the ProjectAddictionCounselor.net website with explanations for functionality and impression.

flair. We don't wanna be boring! A hybrid of convention and creativity is the best formula.

Personal Effects

This blend of creativity and conventionality is imperative. Your office is not only your space. It is your space *and* the clients'. Placing personal items like photos, posters, or trophies in conspicuous places is an obvious attempt to get attention and expresses insecurity. If we do this, we seem desperate to draw attention to ourselves rather than to our clients. Some personal effects should be included in your décor, but not overtly. Personal effects should be there to invite visitors into your world, not to force them.

Your professional documents (e.g., certifications, degrees, awards, and the like) should also be on display for anyone who is curious about your qualifications. Although they should be visible, they should not be the focal point of a room. Making them a focal point also expresses insecurity and a need for validation. As with the personal effects, your documents should not upstage you, the client, or the comfort of the room. I've been in many offices where these documents were so prominent that they seemed to beg for attention. This did not boost my confidence in the service providers; it made me uncomfortable and a little sorry for them, too!

Furniture and Extras

Office furniture should look nice, be functional, and not intimidate anyone. It is difficult for a client to bond with a professional if that professional is clearly at a different level. We want to show that we are successful while simultaneously showing that we're not *too* different: I can understand your plights as a family person and professional, as I live and work in the same community and also work to manage money, family, and personal limitations. I may be successful, but our stations in life are similar.

Be On Time

Clients are allowed to be late, and many of them will be. They are paying for your time, and if they want to pay you for waiting for them, so be it. If a late client apologizes, excuse him or her: "It's OK. This hour belongs to you. Don't worry about it. But we better get busy since we're getting a late start. We've always got lots to cover, and I have someone else coming to see me in an hour."

Be subtle—not judgmental—and place emphasis on service, not tardiness. The words in the example are carefully chosen: saying "I have *someone else* coming" is a deliberate avoidance of the word *client*. Using the word *client*, even about another person, is a reminder that this person is part of your business. It is important to de-emphasize the professional aspect of the relationship and place more emphasis on the personal component. Counseling is not accounting or plumbing: it is an intensely personal service. By de-emphasizing the business aspect, we can maintain the personal one, minimizing awkwardness and feelings of vulnerability.

Never make a client wait for you, and do not make clients feel bad for making you wait. It is not relevant to the work being done (unless that person is coming to you about an addiction to tardiness).

Your being on time is not only professional and considerate, but it also demonstrates virtues and qualities you are trying to instill in your clients. Teach primarily via example, and back up your actions with words, not the other way around.

If you are running late in your sessions, try to text the next client at least twenty to forty-five minutes ahead of time to prevent him or her from having to wait. Apologize and assure the client that the session will be the full time, and then send a message to the next several clients to also advise them you're running behind. Within three or four sessions, you'll able to get back on schedule. You may occasionally need to skip lunch. Time sacrifice is *your* responsibility, not theirs.

While it is somewhat rude to send a text message or receive a call during a session, clients can be accepting and tolerant in certain circumstances. One of the few downsides of being self-reliant is that you have no assistants to intercept calls and handle scheduling details, which means there will be occasional interruptions during sessions. The upside is the affordability of your services as a result of low overhead. If you do need to briefly interrupt a session, you should apologize and thank the client for understanding that the sacrifice he or she makes helps you to be able to provide help to many people at costs most can afford. Most clients will graciously tolerate a few texts per session or a one- to three-minute call interruption unless it is a consistent feature of their sessions. Here is a script for such situations:

"Excuse me a quick moment. I just want to make sure that this text isn't someone in crisis." Then you can look at the message, and if there is not a crisis, put it out of your mind, and deal with it between sessions.

Staying on Schedule

Expect to run late! Many clients are too emotional or self-involved to be attentive to the time during a session, and often they are not receptive to the not-so-subtle hints you're dropping that the session needs to end. Get used to running over and sacrificing your own time.

Through the course of the day and week, it will all work out: you will skim, trim, and edit your duties to compensate. Often when a day's schedule falls behind due to late clients or sessions running over, eventually someone doesn't show at all or leaves early, and the time balances out. While this is not always the case, most of the time the schedule will balance out by the end of the day, as long as you are resourceful and tolerant. You cannot take client's bad time-management skills personally or seriously. By bearing the stress and burden of these errors, you will build your reputation of being cooperative and tolerant, two job requirements for any counselor!

No one likes to wait an hour to see a doctor, yet we all expect to do so. You are not a doctor, and you want your clients to have a positive impression of their experience. With proper time management, no one will ever need to wait for more than ten to fifteen minutes for his or her appointment.

Clocks are an important feature to have in your office. It isn't possible to look at a wristwatch without being noticed, and it is rude, no matter how appropriate it may be. Clocks should be in clear view for you but not visible to the client. Placing a clock behind the client's seat is ideal. I have three clocks in my office. One is just to the right of and behind the main client chair. This one I can see while I look toward the client, without diverting my gaze. The second one is a very small clock that sits on a low coffee-table shelf facing me, away from clients. The third one is more ornate and is off to the side. It is virtually unnoticeable to visiting clients unless they search the room for it. These second two are situated for use during sessions that require me to face the opposite direction of my main client chair. I keep them all five minutes fast so that if a client does see them, he or she will likely wind down his or her time with a few minutes to spare, which allows me to prepare for the next session.

I also recommend investing in a small digital recorder that plugs into your computer's USB port (approximately fifty dollars) and offering to record client sessions. The recorded sessions can easily be transferred through e-mail and are especially useful in hypnotherapy sessions for client playback between sessions, Do not charge extra for this service.

I do not recommend offering snacks, coffee, or drinks to clients (other than water). The counseling office is not a snack bar or restaurant, so do not blur its intent. Clients should be made comfortable, and water should always be easily accessible, as should a restroom. Encourage clients to bring in their own coffee or soda, but do not provide it. Often a client will bring food to a session:

Client: "Do you mind if I eat my bagel while you talk? I haven't eaten. I'm really hungry and want to be able to pay attention. You mind?"

It is awkward to have a serious conversation with anyone while he or she is eating.

Counselor: "No, not at all. You should eat. Tell you what—you take your time and eat, and when you're done, we'll get started. I've got a call I can make, and we'll try to add a few minutes onto our time so we still have what we need. I'll be right back out." With that, I leave the client in my office or waiting area and return in the appropriate amount of time.

We must find a polite way to control the environment while being cooperative and understanding. If we do not control the environment, pace, and direction of the session, we lose credibility: We need to maintain authority. You cannot afford to be passive, aggressive, or passive-aggressive!

Be effectively cooperative and understanding while subtly sending a message that the session is the client's time, and he or she can use it in any way he or she wants: "Talk on your phone, play games, sit in silence—it's your time. How would you like to use it?"

This serves as a reminder to clients that they are spending their money to be there. Essentially it is all the same to you: an hour in exchange for X amount of dollars. Within moments, most people will conclude that they do not wish to spend their resources to have you sit doing nothing while they eat or talk on the phone. (The ones who do are just fine with me: I've always got calls, texts, and e-mails to catch up on and love to get paid during that time.)

The younger a client is, the more latitude you should give. Younger clients are less aware of how their actions affect others and are not usually deliberately imposing.

Maintain control of your environment. The helping field will expose you to people who will test you both professionally and personally. This is a career of consistent exposure to dysfunctional and disordered people. Brace yourself, and set and maintain the space.

Your clients are like guests in your home. Be sure to make them comfortable, and let them know that it is never awkward or rude to need a restroom, check their phone, or excuse themselves—for anything. The more gracious you are about these mildly rude interferences, the less likely most people will be to take advantage of them. There will always be those who are consistently late and interrupt the session with phone calls or other distractions. The message you should convey in demeanor, attitude, or spoken response should be, "It's all right. This is your time, not mine. I would prefer we spent time on the issues you want help with so I can earn what you pay me, but for this hour, I belong to you."

Use subtle firmness to set the tone and control the environment. You must maintain control of the session.

19

MARKETING

Marketing is how we sell; it is the packaging, the expression, and the impression you present to the public. Marketing is how you make the world aware of you—what you can do and why to use you. It is how you become accessible and should include the following:

- branding
- appearance
- advertising
- website
- social media
- developing a platform
- being relevant

Absolutely every interaction a business has with the world is either marketing or antimarketing. You are always making either a good impression or a bad one, but it is not possible to leave no impression. If our impression is good, we are marketing, but if it is forgettable, it is bad (i.e., antimarketing).

As a helping professional, you must assume that you are always on display. The most casual and frivolous conversations may lead to an opportunity for someone to hire you for your services. Everyone on this planet either needs help or knows someone who does. Your role as a counselor is an identity, and it needs to be consistent.

Branding

Much emphasis is placed in this book on being versatile in order to have a wider spectrum of clients and issues to work with. There is also emphasis on specializing.

214

Specializing helps to create a reputation and is a form of branding.

Branding is the way you are identified and differentiated from other professionals and services. You want to be versatile enough to be referred and recommended for a wide variety of issues but known as a specialist in at least one, or a few, particular areas. The name of your practice should concisely describe this. It should be catchy and also express what you offer and do, such as HypnoChange for a hypnotherapy service, Dynamic Strategies for life coaching or counseling, or No Addiction for recovery. Feel free to use these. There are no copyright infringements on public domain labels, and unless a competing service is using a name you want to use, you can and should use it.

It is not advisable to simply go by your first and last name for your practice. Once established and successful with a solid reputation, you can go by Rumpelstiltskin if you want, but until then, a name that invokes is best. No one knows you, so your actual name has no power...yet! It is not identified or automatically associated with your services. Using an invoking name, such as Joe's Cola for a soft drink, is smart marketing. The product is not a mystery because the name invokes your association automatically.

Your practice's name should evoke your mission as well. This can be achieved by using a title and a subtitle. Your practice's name will be on your ads, statements, e-mails, business cards and every other form of media you use. Everything with your name and services on it is exposure for you and your practice. My practice is titled LifeMind and subtitled Change Your Mind, Change Your Life. While there is room for interpretation, the inference evokes specific concepts I want to be associated with. The words *life* and *mind* are abstract yet evoke the nature of the work. The subtitle of "Change your mind, change your life!" says it all. Condensing your mission into a few buzzwords or phrases demonstrates your ability to be economical and effective. Much time should be put into selecting the name and subtitle of your practice (see "Vision").

Until you are known, your name is not evocative to anyone, but over time your name will become synonymous with your work and your practice. No doubt your media (website, ads, and so on) should contain your first and last name, but your practice's title and subtitle should be the most prominent features. It is easy to forget an actual name, but a catchy title can leave an imprint.

Be sure to take advantage of the subtitle of your practice. If the only thing someone reads in your ad or on your card is the banner line, it needs to be as thorough as possible. If your subtitle can get someone's attention, he or she will likely read or look more. First impressions aren't everything, but if you don't get people's attention, they move on quickly. Our society is so inundated with ads and images and other distractions that it's challenging to entice someone to even glance at your ad, let alone form an opinion about it. The current media culture is (as my son put it) the Snapchat, Instagram, 30-second, 140-character generation, attention spans are waning and diminishing very quickly as a result.

You're encouraged to read some basics on marketing. *Wikipedia*, Twitter, YouTube, and Facebook have lots to review.

Appearance

There is an entire section devoted to the subject of appearance because it is significant and can easily go wrong, in spite of our best intentions and good taste. Your appearance should be your own—unique and individual—yet it should also be conventional enough to make nearly everyone confident in and comfortable with you. Your appearance should never be the focal point of who you are as a professional. Looking smart, effective, fashionable, stylish, and comfortable is the priority. It is easy to overdo—or underdo—your style, which then affects client volume. Appearance is part of your marketing. The way you look is an expression of who you are. Carefully read and apply the "Appearance" chapter in this book.

Advertising

Advertising is expensive and can quickly bankrupt you. Advertising locally is the only option, as a national magazine (such as *Time* or *People*) is unlikely to produce local clients who can attend sessions, besides being far too expensive to advertise with. Let's review the marketing mediums and how to maximize each.

Print

Print mediums are magazines and newspapers[17]. I recommend local publications, which are typically small, that reach your community area. Most people are unwilling to drive far for regular sessions, as there are always closer options. It is better to try to advertise with a local magazine rather than a local newspaper. Magazines address local shopping, services, and events in a more dynamic way. They may have fewer readers than local newspapers, but readers are more likely to respond to the content.

Local classifieds have a stigma, making them inappropriate for this particular field. Classifieds are for jobs, rentals, and services like babysitting or housepainting, not counseling. If you go to Craigslist and click on the "Therapist" tab, you'll see nothing but massage services. While you may get noticed and even get some calls from a classified listing, many people who see you there will categorize you as garage-sale counseling, and the small amount of exposure and few clients you get are not worth tarnishing your image.

---

[17] I have included several print ads at the end of this section for review.

Most local magazines have a calendar section that lists local events, and it is usually free to list events there. This is where you can announce your free workshops. It is very effective if readers see your workshop notice and your formal print ad in the same magazine issue.

Most local magazines have several issues a year with feature sections that highlights topics such as plumbing, kitchen remodeling, self-help, or family services. These are usually one- to three-page inserts that list professionals who offer these services. My local magazine has an annual medical issue that allows advertisers to list their names and a brief description of what they do. While I'm not a doctor, my services qualify. If you time a workshop near one of these feature issues, you'll have great exposure: your regular ad combined with the featured listing and a workshop listed in the calendar section. This makes a powerful impression of being accessible and engaged in the community. With the expense of only your ad, you appear three times in that issue.

Try to seek out magazines that have advertorials. An advertorial is a 200- to 500-word editorial that accompanies your ad, allowing you to elaborate on your services. An advertorial appears as an editorial to the reader, as it addresses a specific issue (e.g., drugs or hypnotherapy). You are given credit for the editorial, and your credentials are listed. I've included a sample of one of mine at the end of this section. Advertorials are a current marketing trend and are very effective. I am confident this trend will become a norm.

The magazine advertorial format is powerful, and I can honestly say that it is the most effective form of advertising that exists. A print ad, no matter how great, does not give you the opportunity to introduce yourself or to demonstrate your skill and knowledge. The magazine I am with is 90 percent advertorial content. The advertorial is powerful ad media. Readers are exposed to vendors in far more detail, making this a win for the merchant, the customer/reader, and the publication.

Nearly every community has a local print medium, whether it is a local paper, newspaper, or magazine.[18] A publication that is available only within your community gives you the opportunity to channel the ad toward relevant, topical issues. Buzzwords to feature are addiction, recovery, fitness, weight loss, and smoking cessation. You should also clearly offer services for "personal growth and self-improvement" in "all areas." In a family-oriented community, your ad may list issues such as youth's performance in sports and education. These common self-improvement treatments can fill out a schedule, and offering them is a good way to build your skills, reputation, and confidence.

However, these issues do not have longevity. If you are good at your job, those issues will get resolved in three to six sessions, and if you're not good at your job, clients will move on even sooner. If your services are versatile, clients will stay with you to work on other relevant issues.

Addiction treatment gets the attention of anyone and everyone affected by it and will bring calls.

It is advisable to run two ads if this is affordable. The ads should be different: one ad should combine hypnotherapy, life-coaching services, and other alternative services, and you should have a separate ad for addiction counseling. Drug-counseling clients may never know you have other services, and people who see you for self-improvement issues may never know you offer drug counseling. Some will be aware of both. Keep your services separate so as not to inadvertently scare clients or have them draw wrong conclusions. Many people looking for life coaching or hypnotherapy may feel conflicted about seeing a drug counselor for what they need. (Addiction clients, on the other hand, will have no issue with your providing other

---

[18] To confirm this, I went online and typed in two random cities with *newspaper* after their name. The two I typed (Bend, Oregon, and Marion, Ohio) both have their own local newspaper with classifieds. Both also sell advertising and have calendar sections for local events. These are small towns.

services.) It is not necessary to lie or hide your other services; it is simply better to be discreet about them.

Over time, as you build trust and rapport with clients and your community, they will get to know your work in other areas, and it will gain appreciation and recognition. It is natural to occasionally refer to other cases and challenges in varying contexts. You can, will, and should use examples of and references to other cases—including personal struggles, successes, and failures—to accent points and strategies.

Your openness about your other work and your personal life should be proportionate to the rapport you have with a given client. We don't share details of our personal lives in casual conversations with a neighbor or a grocery clerk; the details we share about our lives are different for everyone we know and based on the context and nature of the relationship. We may be very close to our children, but we certainly do not share details about our romantic relationships, especially regarding intimacy. It would be inappropriate and would make us (and them) feel awkward and uncomfortable. And I don't want to know about my kid's sex life, either!

Not only is it advisable to run separate ads for your specific services, but the ads should look slightly different as well. Your ads should have a theme that is identifiable as yours, yet the two should not have the exact same images. If someone passed on an earlier ad because he didn't feel it was relevant to him, he will automatically assume the second ad is the exact same, even though it's not. The graphics and layout can be similar, but they should have a slightly different look. The end of this section includes samples of actual ads.

Buzzwords

Ambiguous buzzwords can be interpreted by many people in many different ways, widening the scope of your offered services: your ad might say, "Build Confidence," "Break Habits," "Live to Your Potential," or "Reduce

Stress." When people see a word or phrase that resonates with them, they feel a sense of kismet, as though fate has intervened.

An ad should be descriptive and stylish, yet clear. Be careful not to crowd the space with too much imagery or text. People are easily overwhelmed by crowded ads and often skip over them. If there is not enough content, on the other hand, they are left trying to unravel the mystery of the aim of the ad, which is not worth their time, so they move on.

You need to find a concise, graceful design, and this balance is not easy. It is tempting to hire an ad designer, and many publications include free help if you advertise with them. But hired designers can be expensive. While they have talent and experience with advertising, it is imperative you lead the process by guiding the ad designer to what your service is and what you want to convey. I recommend attempting to design your own ad first. See what you're capable of before you decide to hire a professional.

I had a consult with a magazine's ad designer and told him what I did professionally. "I'm a hypnotherapist and help people to realize their goals and make changes in their lives" was how I described it. He drafted an ad of a woman diving into a backyard swimming pool. My name, practice name, phone number and new motto—Change Your Mind, Change Your Life—were all prominently displayed.

I could not understand how this ad even remotely pertained to what I actually do: I do not teach swimming, nor do I install pools. When I asked the ad designer what it meant or how it related to what I do, he didn't have much of an answer, either. So I drafted my own. Below is a copy of the very first ad I used as a hypnotherapist, prior to becoming a private-practice counselor:

This ad received moderate response. I was brand new and one of two hypnotherapists advertising in the magazine.

Eight months later, I designed a new ad: a photo of a woman (my girlfriend) sitting peacefully in a relaxed, meditative pose on a rustic hillside with a view of our community valley below and the sun on the horizon. The image was peaceful, and the setting conveyed beauty and nature, both of which invoke serenity and possibility. It was a decent start, and it at least made some sense. I modified it every month by a word or two for several months.

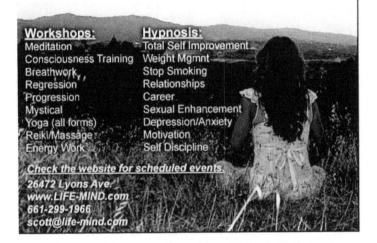
This was stylish and evocative to a specific audience—women and to those receptive to a slightly New Age perspective. While that's a large market, it does not access much of the male population or women in general. The demographic is powerful and lucrative but limited.

I received adequate response from this ad. Six months later, I went with a reverse-copy ad:

Reverse copy is a reliable tool. It is not glamorous and lacks creativity, but the directness is hard to miss: "less is more" is often the best approach. Next, I began my first advertising for drug-counseling services (next page). I used these for several years and got a great response.

224

Response to this ad increased about 30 percent almost immediately. As I review the two now, a bit older and wiser and with a tad more business acumen, I can see the faults more clearly: these ads contain too much text. Had I put more thought into consolidating and simplifying the material, the ads would have had a cleaner look and not given an impression of being complex. They were adequate, but they could be improved—a lot![19]

---

[19] Note that my title in each was Life Counselor, and in one edition I listed myself as a licensed counselor. A local professional, likely a competitor, complained to the magazine that *licensed* was an inappropriate term, as was *life counselor*. I altered them to avoid professional misconduct and misrepresentation.

After five years of running the reverse-copy ads, I changed them again. I was happy with the reverse-copy ads and the response I got from them; however, it is important to change, evolve, and stay fresh. I created my last incarnation:

While I like and prefer the last incarnation, I acknowledge that it would not have been the best vehicle for me in the

---

[20] These ads were $295 per month. The cost would have been more had the ads been in color, which I was unwilling to pay. In 2010, the magazine went all color at no additional cost. To see all the samples in color visit ProjectAddictionCounselor.net.

226

beginning of my practice. The reverse-copy ad was appropriate for starting out; it was simple and no-frills. After my reputation was solid and my practice was strong, I was free to be more creative and stylish. After five years, it was important to show a fresh look to the community. The fresh look showed that I was evolving, stable, and engaged in my business. A new, fresh look is vital; even Coca-Cola™ changes its design to stay relevant and fresh.

Business Cards

The average cost of good-quality double-sided business cards is between forty and seventy dollars for one thousand. I recommend double-sided cards so you can include more content without overwhelming the face of the card. The cost difference between double-sided cards and one-sided cards is minimal and worth the investment. You will see by reviewing my samples what the format is: contact information and other vital information go on the front, with bullet points listing services on the back. The theme is consistent, yet the front cannot be mistaken for the back.

While it is tempting to print cards at home, the cost of professional printing is only slightly higher, but the increase in quality will be noticeable. A business card is often your first impression, so it needs to be effective. To save money I instruct my printer to give me a gloss finish on the front (more expensive) and a matte finish on the back. Using the matte finish on the back saves me about twenty dollars per order and does not compromise content or consistency. Use the same or similar content and images from your print ads to strengthen your brand and be consistent.

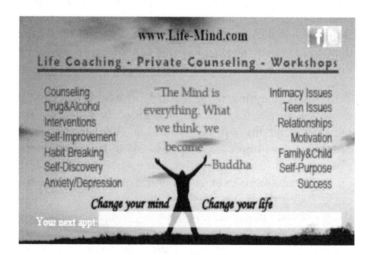

It is a good idea to leave a space on the back of your business cards to write in a client's next appointment time. If you give these to clients as reminders, your cards will be dispersed everywhere. Clients will lose them on the bus and drop them in their cars. Many of my clients have dozens of my cards polluting their houses, which means they are seen by every family member and friend who visits them. My cards are all over my community, and I get several calls each year from people who found my card at a friend's house or on a bus bench or don't even know how they ended up with it.

In addition to that, the space on the back gives my clients a written reminder of their next appointment. My contract states that full payment is due if a client misses an appointment without proper cancellation, so a written record prevents disputes about the actual time. When a client insists that I had the time wrong, I humorously ask him or her to produce the card. If I was wrong, I apologize, make it a joke, and reschedule. If the card confirms I was right, the client is obligated to pay for the missed appointment. If clients lose the card, it is the same as being wrong, and they pay. While it can be a bit uncomfortable or awkward at times, overall this system is efficient yet informal and has caused many laughs. I've been wrong about scheduled times and days about 25 percent of the time. Using the cards as appointment reminders requires each client to take a card at the end of each session which is how your cards end up littered all over the community.

Brochures

Brochures are not required in the beginning, but they are almost an expected medium. A brochure creates an appearance of success. The cost is relatively low, and the brochure is an expansive way to promote your services. When I first started out, I printed trifold brochures at home: they were crude. At that time, doing so was appropriate. I wasn't willing to invest much, as I didn't see much opportunity to dispense them. I promoted my sessions and workshops by my presence and presentations and business cards, and I knew that most people would throw brochures in the trash minutes after receiving them (I do). It wasn't until I was comfortable and stable that I had good-quality color brochures printed. I always have a good quantity on hand, and I make them available at workshops and appearances and display them in my office, but even after events with dozens of people, I only seem to go through a very small and insignificant number of them. They are good to have on hand and, at my status, a necessary and expected marketing tool, but overall they are impractical, as the cost is disproportionate to the response to them. Samples are included for review.

As you begin, invest in good-quality business cards and brochures only if you have the resources. Once you are established, you can invest in them more seriously. Here are two samples of tri-fold brochures (top images: exterior, bottom image: interior).

Full size images are on the ProjectAddictionCounselor.net website[21].

---

[21] Customizable templates for print ads, advertorials, business cards, tri-folds, website and workshops are available to all Project Addiction/LifeMind counselors. Go to www.ProjectAddictionCounselor.net

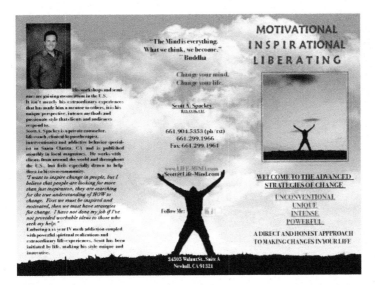

- *ADVANCED*
- *EFFECTIVE*
- *HONEST*

THERE IS A SCIENCE TO TRANSFORMATION. LET IT *EMPOWER* YOU!

"There seems to be an unseen force that keeps me from making the changes in myself I truly need to make."

We know what we want to be and often we even know what to do. Yet... we cannot seem to get past the unseen force. That unseen force is your own subconscious mind. It is compelled to hold behaviors in place, even ones that could hold us back and do us harm.

WHY?

There are principles that drive the mind; rules and laws, that are powerful and fixed. If we are to change the way we act or think, we must get the support of our subconscious because the conscious decision to change is clearly not enough.

HOW?

Knowledge is power. True understanding is the first stage to successful change. You must understand how it works if you are to become the master over your own mind &... your life.

But what's next?

Once we have true understanding we must be properly motivated and inspired. We know we want to change and that until we do we are in a state of suffering.

But isn't there more? YES!

True motivation is a clear, faithful, personal understanding of why we need, require & must have, these changes if we are ever to be fulfilled. Having a superficial reasoning is not enough. Until we have a *cathartic* experience our desire for change remains ultimately dormant and impotent, not powerful enough to truly act. We fall again and again.

What exactly is catharsis?

A catharsis is a feeling of being purified emotionally, spiritually, or psychologically as a result of an intense emotional experience. It triggers a *paradigm shift (a radical change in perception)* and your reasons to change come into focus in an intense way, triggering action and finally the strength, courage and commitment to do what must be done.

Okay... let's say I'm motivated properly, but I still may not know how to proceed with change, then what?

Strategies are vital to change. Most of the methods you need are already within... locked away in your subconscious, waiting to be revealed and set free. Once you are properly motivated they will be released.

In my workshops, seminars and sessions I work closely with clients to bring those strategies forth and you are trained and taught how to problem solve and create working strategies for success in every area of your life, unlocking your own inner potential.

The Alchemy of Change:

Alchemy refers to the transformation of the human spirit and the sequences we must go through for change to be permanent rather than temporary.

If we attempt to skip or avoid these very natural sequences, our changes will be temporary and superficial.

In my workshops, seminars and sessions I guide and mentor you through these sequences. They are profound, insightful and often mystical. I bring a lifetime of study and experience drawing from psychology, philosophy, spirituality and personal insight to enlighten others.

Whatever you desire, whatever you hope to achieve, you can! Don't let life pass you by. Become enlightened!

Every workshop, seminar & session is designed to liberate you from what binds you. I am intensely passionate about the process of change— I'm in love with it.

Witnessing the suffering of others inspires me to find solutions and enlighten those who might be stuck.

I've traveled the world in search of truths and grew up in difficult circumstances that have initiated me to levels of awareness and perspective that others seem to miss.

Addiction recovery, parenthood, owning two successful businesses, finding true love for life, working for years with those in need of change and having profound spiritual realizations has taught me to focus on humility & compassion, yet not lose any intensity in my desire to lead others to their highest potential. I hope you will join me soon for a life-changing experience!

Marketing Pace

Car companies Kia and Hyundai were synonymous with low-budget cars and were not considered by executive and upper-class buyers. They started out small and appealed to economical buyers in the beginning. But in 2012 they produced the Optima and the Sonata, respectively. They did not stop offering economy cars. Nor did Toyota when it came out with the Camry, which changed its reputation. These car companies built a strong foundation and powerful capital *before* they ventured into the higher-performance luxury-sedan market.

Pace yourself: start small and slow, and gain experience in both service skills and business acumen. Remember that slow and steady wins the race. If you want to have longevity for your career, take your time and grow reasonably. Pace cost and marketing strategies.

Website

Build a website. Now.

Well? Go do it!

A website is inexpensive, and your print ad, business cards, presentations, brochures, and flyers can direct people to it. Your website is *your* domain, and no editor is allowed to limit your content or word count! You can have entire pages that describe topics, methods, and strategies, along with many images—there are few limitations. A website is essential if you hope to be taken seriously. Each time I am introduced to a business, the first thing I (or anyone) will do is visit its site to determine whether it is the right company. We all want details, and websites make this information accessible. This is the digital age, and you better text and have a smartphone, a tablet, a laptop, *and* a website! All of them!

A website is an expression of who you are and an opportunity to pitch sales. It is often the first impression you will make on a prospective client. Your website is your opportunity to introduce yourself in as much detail as you want. A large percentage of clients found me by searching keywords such as *drug counseling* and *hypnotherapy*. They did not meet me at a presentation, nor were they referred by a friend. They did a search and my site came up, and they liked what they saw and how it was communicated and presented.

I went to a drug symposium and the organizers were kind enough to list all the vendor participants on handouts that were given to all who attended. Out of twenty-five participants, fifteen were city or county facilities, and the other ten were private organizations and programs, including myself. Each vendor had his or her name, contact number, and website listed. Five of the ten (of which I was one) had working websites, but the other five did not. I searched for all five: two were "under construction," and the other three did not exist at all. In the digital age, a website is as imperative as clothing! It's more than expected—you can't be taken seriously without it!

As with the print ads, you should try to design the website yourself. For less than seventy dollars, you can buy quality web hosting for a year. Web-hosting services include web-building templates that you can change, modify, and add to as you grow. You don't need to be computer proficient to do it, as it is all intuitive. Try to use your web host's service tools and customer service to diffuse problems, and take your time to let your site evolve. The first version of my website was pretty cool— for an amateur—and the one you will visit today is still my own creation. No doubt it can be better and more professional, but it is as good—even better—than many. Be patient. It's best to draft and design your website before you open your practice so you can work on it for a few hours each week. By the time you open for business, it will have evolved!

Refrain from crowded templates and images and designs that cause your message to get lost. You may love puppy dogs or baseball, but these are not relevant designs or images. Leave the personal touches to your Instagram, Facebook, or Twitter pages.

Social Media

Social media is a great marketing tool, and your practice should use it. If you have a personal social-media account, it is best to run two: one for your personal contacts and one for your practice.

Twitter, Facebook, Instagram, Snapchat, LinkedIn—these are important tools, and time should be invested in them—marginally. It is easy to get caught up in the social-media web, as many people use it to simply pass time. Do not be seduced by the disproportionate promise of social media. It is a good tool, and it is imperative to stay relevant and digitally visible, but you should not invest in it exclusively. Each social medium should be posted to or interacted with two to five times per week—but no more. It is easy to get overexposure through social media. While we are initially drawn in by someone who is new and interesting, it is natural to feel complacent to anything we're overexposed to. Social-media posts should be topical, relevant, and interesting. No one (nope—not even your family) cares about mundane, meaningless information like what you had for dinner or that you went to the beach. Think about what *you* read on social-media sites and what you skip over. It is easy to be caught up in a moment and feel an impulse to post and share the experience. When this happens, wait a few hours, and see if it's still relevant. If it is, then post it. If the feeling has passed, skip it.

Two to five posts per week is about as interesting as anyone's life is. Rock stars lead pretty hedonistic lives, and pretty extraordinary, too, but if we are exposed to their happenings every day, even that becomes complacent and boring. Be present enough that people know you exist,

235

but not so present that they take you for granted. All of us already have people we take for granted and need to feign interest in; don't be one of them.

I'm not the best adviser on this subject, as I get so busy creating things and providing services that I don't have time to use social media. If I am too busy in my personal life and my practice is so lucrative that I barely have time to use social media, that's a good thing! Be careful it does not end up a distraction from work needing your attention. If you do good work and provide powerful things, you will get support and attention and become known. It is a relevant argument that social media can improve business, but virtual reality can also distract you from doing real work. Both are important, so commit time to regularly use social media, but not too frequently.

With the right services, you can link your social-media accounts. I can create posts on a Monday and have them timed to be released on all of my media on Friday at ten o'clock in the morning. Nina Amir's *How to Blog a Book* explains precisely how to effectively create a platform using social media.[22] While it focuses on blogging, it explains many other modalities and provides lists of links and services.

Everything and anything you print on social media should be professionally appropriate. As counselors, we are potentially subjected to the court of public opinion. Whether you're at the grocery store or on Facebook or Twitter, you are always on display. You need to be cautious and conscious that your expressions do not depart from your image as a counselor. Your private life should be just that: private. There is a difference between your personal life and your private life. Your private life should never be displayed on social media. You should keep your social-media presence real and personal, but nothing you post should make anyone uncomfortable about you. A

---

[22] *Platform* is synonymous with self-promotion and public relations.

counselor is on the job always. If you're doing something that would or could embarrass you—something you're not proud of—maybe it's not something you should be doing in the first place.

Soft Sell

Very few people are attracted to the hard-sell personality, even though it works well in specific industries. A helping professional cannot risk coming on strong or appearing imposing. We need to weave our services into conversations. We should not miss the opportunity to market during social events, such as barbecues, kids' sports practices, or back-to-school nights, but we must be subtle.

In a social climate, look for an opportunity to provide information or an insight to a person, and then follow with an example. Only when asked should we disclose what we do for a career. Lead people to the question subtly, not overtly. The formula is as follows: a positive followed by a negative followed by a positive (P+N+P). Let's eavesdrop on a casual conversation taking place at a barbecue:

Mrs. C: "Yeah, my job is stressful, but I love my job, and it provides for my family."

You: "Me too. I think stress is an important feature of one's career and of life. As uncomfortable as it may be, we're setting the example of hard work as a virtue for our kids. Working hard sends a message to our kids: work, stress, and managing family are not only possible, but necessary. You're living the example. You can be proud."

Mrs. C: "True. I worry about quality time, though. Even when I'm with the kids or my husband, I'm not always present. You know what I mean?"

You: "I do. It seems impossible to wear all the hats. It can feel overwhelming. Managing family, finances, a career, and romance takes artful compartmentalizing!"

237

Mrs. C: "Yes, it does. It does get overwhelming. It seems no matter what we do, there's always more to be done."

You: "Yes, and it's natural to feel exhausted and tense. I've been helping a client for several weeks with this exact issue. We built strategies together for her to manage responsibilities better and sleep better to feel less overwhelmed. What surprised me was that the work made *me* practice what I was preaching, and I feel better now, too!"

Mrs. C: "Oh, is that what you do for a living? Are you like a doctor or a therapist?"

You: "I'm more of a coach and consultant, but yeah. I teach and train people to improve and achieve their goals—no matter what they are—and this woman's goal was to feel less stressed without cutting her responsibilities. Her responsibilities are important to her. If we could all just walk away from our responsibilities, that'd be easy, but we would die of guilt and heartache from abandoning those we love and the things we want to achieve. So I went outside the box and advised her to keep all her responsibilities. Now she's learning how to compartmentalize them better. I'm proud of her. She's really progressed."

Now let's examine what occurred:

Mrs. C: "Yeah, my job is stressful, but I love my job, and it provides for my family."

- This is the "presenting issue" that needs attention.

You: "Me too. I think stress is an important feature of one's career and of life. As uncomfortable as it may be, we're preparing our children for facts of life: work, stress, and managing family, too. And we're doing it by example. You can be proud." (Positive)

- You've identified and validated the issue.

238

Mrs. C: "True, I worry about quality time, though. Even when I'm with the kids or my husband, I'm not always present. You know what I mean?"

You: "I do. It seems impossible to wear all the hats. It can feel overwhelming." (Negative) Managing family, finances, a career, and romance takes artful compartmentalizing!" (Positive)

- You are identifying and validating again.

Mrs. C: "Yes, it does. It does get overwhelming. It seems no matter what we do, there's always more to be done."

You: "Yes, and it's natural to feel exhausted and tense."

- You are validating her experience and branding it ("exhausted and tense").

You: I've been helping a client for several weeks with this exact issue. Not only did we build strategies together for her to manage better and sleep better to feel less overwhelmed, but the work made *me* practice what I was preaching, and I feel better, too!"

- You are providing bait to invite inquiry. You are also teasing about results and providing self-verification of them.
  Note: If no inquiry is made at this point, leave it as a casual conversation, and do not reemphasize.

Mrs. C: "Oh, is that what you do for a living? Are you like a doctor or a therapist?"

You: "I'm more of a coach and consultant, but yeah. I teach and train people to improve and achieve their goals—no matter what they are—and this woman's goal was to feel less stressed without cutting out any of her responsibilities. Her responsibilities are important to her. If we could all just walk away from our responsibilities that'd be easy, but we would die of the guilt and heartache of abandoning those we love and things we want to achieve. She didn't want to take medication, and her first

239

therapist recommended she simply needed to do less. So I went outside the box and advised her to keep all her responsibilities, and she is learning how to compartmentalize them better."

- If an inquiry is made, you can provide a brief description of your work while subtly implying that what you provide is smarter and better than other available options. The implication is that one would have to be conventional and dumb *not* to want such help!

Let's rejoin the conversation:

Mrs. C: "Yeah, I don't want meds, either. And I certainly can't quit my job or my family! I guess we just have to deal with it."

- This is an indication the person is not interested, as no further inquiry about your services was made. Make a parting shot that is subtle:

You: "Well, if you're interested in the outside-the-box ideas—no meds—I don't mind sharing a few ideas with you over the phone or through e-mail. No charge, I promise. Take my card. It'd only take me a few minutes, and I'd be happy to. Really."

- By offering your card but not asking for her number, you have not obligated or intimidated the potential client. You have invited dialogue and communication. If she does not contact you, you've invested nothing. If she does, you invest time. Be careful, as many people will take advantage of that free service, exploiting your time with phone calls or e-mails.
- After a few e-mails, invite the person to a session by explaining that the subject is just too complicated to convey via e-mail. She will either stop contacting you or make an appointment. She may even refer someone.

- I've had new clients who were referred to me several months before they called. I've had clients who contacted me a whole year after seeing one of my presentations or workshops. I've had clients who were referred to me by someone I met at a barbecue! You never know if, how, or when an impression may pay off, so you should treat everyone like a potential client. Be respectful and considerate, but always be comfortable setting your own boundaries, too.

My very first hypnotherapy client is still a client after ten years. I met this person at a social event (a family barbecue with my in-laws). A group of people were gathering outside the house to smoke. I approached them and slipped in the fact that I was a hypnotherapist into the conversation. Within minutes one woman asked if it could truly help with smoking. "Of course!" I replied. I handed out a few cards and then entirely changed the subject. She called in a week, and we began a smoking-cessation program. Once her smoking behavior was resolved, she continued seeing me as a personal coach and counselor. It has been my honor to participate in her growth and self-evolution all these years.

Soft Sell Dos and Don'ts

DO: Look for opportunities in social settings to introduce your services.

DON'T: Create those opportunities.

DO: Answer questions and give free advice.

DON'T: Persist on any topic. Less is more, and it's best to always leave people wanting more.

Platform

Platform is the term used for the whole spectrum of exposure and accessibility: a website, a social-media presence, seminars, appearances, blogs, workshops, advertising, and so on.

If we devote time to each and every platform medium, we will never sleep or do our job. Print advertising, websites, and workshops are the most effective ways to develop a platform, as these mediums allow people to build a relationship with you quickly and do not dominate your time. Print ads and websites can display your photo and describe you and what you do in a soft sell: people can click (or not) or read (or turn the page). Workshops allow you to demonstrate your skills and build a relationship with participants in person. Each person who attends your free workshop is already interested in your services, and the actual workshop can close the deal.

Workshops

Public Workshops and Presentations

It is recommended that you offer free workshops about community issues (like drug use) to your local city council. Most communities have a city council that is looking for professionals to run free workshops. Not only will the council promote the workshops, but it will provide the venue, which saves you the expense. You may want to reach out to local council members by phone, e-mail, or letter to explore and offer. Below is a suggested message.

I've been a resident of this community for five years and always want to give back and make a contribution. I am a hypnotherapist/life coach/addiction counselor and often do workshops and presentations on issues to teach people usable strategies to improve and succeed in life. I work with kids, teens, business professionals, families, moms, dads—you name it! It would be an honor to provide a free workshop for the community. I'm including a list of topics for your review, but feel free to suggest a topic you feel is more appropriate and needed. If I can do it, I will! I hope to hear from you, and thanks so much for your time.

Hopefully, this initiates a dialogue between you and a city administrator. If you get no reply, follow up in a week to ten days. If there is still no reply, let it go: they're not interested.

With this style of reaching out, I have been asked to provide workshops for my city on a dozen occasions. I have only acquired about five clients over the years from those workshops, but the city administrators all know of me, and several have referred me. In addition, the publicity is valuable, and the experience looks great on a resume. I also gain excellent experience in conducting workshops, and it is a charitable thing to do, which feels great! Providing workshops for the city also got me invited to join a city-council committee with several other professionals (physicians, law-enforcement officers, school administrators, and teachers). The committee met twice per month to discuss community issues and brainstorm ways to improve the community. This has been fulfilling and challenging and has provided powerful networking opportunities.

Private Workshops and Presentations

There are presentation spaces to rent in every community, such as recreation rooms, libraries, conference rooms in office buildings, and others. They all cost money, so you should be cautious when looking for potential sites. Apply these ideas to your community, and be resourceful:

- As a member of a local public gym, I had access to an event room for free, twice per year. If I wanted to use it more than twice, the fee was $150. The room was stylish and comfortable. Many facilities will rent out space to nonmembers as well.
- You can also reach out to friends, neighbors, and family members who may be executives or work in an office. Ask if their office building has a conference room. Can they access it? Anyone who assists in acquiring a space can be compensated

with an invitation to the workshop, a free session, or lunch.

- Many office buildings rent out conference rooms to nontenants. Call your local building-management companies.
- Most cities have recreation rooms and community centers that are very nice but a little expensive. Check them out and compare.
- A recreation room at a nice condo complex or apartment building is adequate.
- Hotels all have rentable spaces.

Be resourceful. It is very likely you can set up a few workshops with little to no expense.

Workshop Structure

A workshop should be more than an hour and no more than ninety minutes with a ten-minute break two-thirds of the way through[23].

It is advisable to offer workshops for free in the beginning. You may add a suggested donation amount to your notices or flyers. Most people will happily donate something and look at the donation as an admission fee, and that's great. You don't want to exclude those who might not be able to afford a minimal fee or are simply unwilling to commit for a fee. You've dedicated the time and venue already, so it is better to present to a full room of free attendees than to present to a nearly empty room for twenty dollars in revenue.

It is advisable to schedule two days/times for the same workshops: one weekday evening and one weekend midday. Many people who may want to attend are not available on weekends, and vice versa. Schedule both, and

---

[23] The Project Addiction and LifeMind trainees are provided with workshop content including outlines. These include full templates, bullet points and slide shows.

be prepared to present twice. Many times, however, one workshop will get a high registration, while the second won't. For example, ten people may register for the weekend workshop, but only one may register for the weekday evening. If this occurs, you should contact the lone registrant and try to persuade him or her to attend the other workshop to avoid a second presentation for only one person: "Hi, I'm e-mailing about the upcoming workshop on Thursday, May 2. Unfortunately, the Thursday workshop may get canceled due to low registration, but the weekend one will be presented for sure. Would it be possible for you to attend on the weekend? I truly apologize and would like to invite you as my guest, free of charge. If not, I will see if I can reschedule to do it another time."

In most instances, that person will not be available for the other workshop, which is why he or she signed up for the one they did. Then you need to make a choice: cancel or present to one person, which is awkward for both of you! The only other option is to reach out to the weekend registrants and ask them to switch days, which is rather impractical.

Statistically, the best weekend times and days are Saturdays after noon but before four. Many people have commitments on weekend mornings and evenings, especially those with kids. Sundays do not get high volumes at all. Weekday workshops are best on Tuesdays, Wednesdays, and Thursdays. Mondays are committed to adjusting to the workweek after weekends, and Fridays are for preparing for weekends. Many classes and programs (yoga, aerobics, bowling, and so on) meet on Tuesdays or Wednesdays, thereby competing with your workshop. It is unlikely that someone who already has a standing commitment to a program will be willing to skip it for your workshop. Experiment and see which days work best in your community. Weekday times are best at seven or seven thirty. People need time to return from work, address household issues, eat something, shower or change, and drive to you workshop. If it is earlier than seven, some may register to come but change their mind due to the stress of making time and room. If your workshop begins later than eight o'clock, it won't end until nine thirty or ten, and many people want to be home at an early hour to settle in and comfortably prepare for the next day. Each community is different: in Manhattan, you may want to start at ten o'clock at night, and in a quiet, sleepy suburb, you may need to begin by six.

Style and Format

Use visual aids to accentuate your presentation (such as a PowerPoint slide show). This is professional, shows creativity, and keeps people visually stimulated. Do not *rely* on visual aids, but use them. The content of your workshop should be presented verbally with only five to ten images to accompany the narrative content. It is easy to get distracted with the need to perform, but it is the content that should truly be the substance. Your presentation should be attractive and dynamic, but it should not upstage the content or concept.

Never read a speech from a script: you are presenting a workshop, not a speech. Outline a few topics and keep index cards nearby, but speak off the cuff. Even if your content gets a little lost or you lose your place, no one will notice since they do not know what it's supposed to be in the first place. Visual aids will serve to remind you of what to elaborate on and when. After each slide and subtopic, always ask if there are questions. This activates audience participation and interaction and allows you to elaborate and improvise. Asking whether there are any questions also breaks the pace slightly, which is essential. Keep question responses brief, but not too brief. Any question (or questioner) that deserves or requires more time can be addressed later to keep the program on track: "What a great topic and question. I hope I addressed it, but I feel that particular topic deserves more attention. If you—and anyone else—want to hang out a bit after, I'll go into it more, no problem."

Do not offer snacks. Doing so detracts from your credibility and the theme of your presentation. Make sure water, tea, and coffee are available, but nothing else.

Advise everyone where the restrooms are, and encourage them to get up for coffee, tea, water, or the restroom at any time: "No need to wait or be polite. Help yourself."

Remember to set the guests at ease: "Please feel free to text or do anything you need during this. It won't bother me, and you're my guest, so be comfortable. It's not rude, so be at home here!" Actually, it *is* rude, but by calling out such behavior before it happens and giving your approval, you're using reverse psychology. Most people who do such things won't. Those who do will be brief and maybe even excuse themselves outside.

Begin five minutes after the scheduled start time, and end on time. Even if the room is empty, you should begin five minutes after schedule. Five minutes is considerate to late arrivals, but anything more is inconsiderate to those who arrived on time. Welcome latecomers, and offer to summarize what they missed during the break. Or, if you prefer, you can choose not to acknowledge them, allowing them to take a seat. This way, you do not interrupt your topic or risk embarrassing them.

You should have a sign-in sheet at the entrance. Point it out, but do not ask the attendees to add to it. If they want to, they will, and if they don't, they won't. The registration sheet should be on your letterhead with formatted lines, and a few pens and blank sheets of paper should be available for anyone who wants to take notes during your workshop. Do not tether a pen or pencil to your sign-in clipboard. It looks cheap (because it is). Buy a box of cheap pens, and expect to lose some.

Below is a typical sign-in sheet format:

Name	Address/City	Phone	E-mail

Be sure to mention that signing in is not required or necessary and that the most they will receive from you is a notice of future workshops—nothing else. You might also mention that you'd appreciate it if no one would solicit *you*, either.

Finally, do not perform. Present and speak conversationally. A workshop is not a show. If you stay in your comfort zone, people will warm up to you, and vice versa. You are not expected or required to be a great public speaker. You are giving relevant information for free (or for a fee), and those who come will be grateful.

You'll get better over time. Because I am an introvert, speaking and giving workshops are not my most comfortable marketing tools, but I love my knowledge and my work. Once the ball gets rolling, I lose myself in the concepts and soon forget about the performance aspect. Do what you know, and share from your passion, allowing it to guide you.

It is natural to be nervous, and you should not waste energy trying to *stop* being nervous. Coexist with the nerves. Accept nervousness, and do your best in spite of it. Remember that the majority of people are absorbed in their own thoughts and concerns and are not aware of your nervousness. Don't *try* to relax: own your nervousness. You'd be weird if you weren't nervous! You're standing in front of a group strangers and need to entertain and inform them. Nervousness is normal! If you are an introvert, you will not enjoy presenting, but enjoyment is not required. Be self-forgiving—it's natural and perfectly normal to feel uncomfortable and wish for it to be over. If you're an extrovert, you may enjoy presenting very much.

Either way, you will need to step out of your comfort zone: introverts need to be more expressive than is natural for them, and extroverts may need to tone it down a bit. Your audience will consist of both—introverts and extroverts. Therefore it is best to be in the middle: personable and friendly (extroverted) and gentle and approachable (introverted).

TV and Radio

Some communities have local radio or television channels, and most of them are desperate for interesting content. They are inundated with real-estate agents and retail businesses and have few opportunities to present helpful, dynamic guests or vital information that isn't provided by local officials. You don't need to have model good looks or a supercharming personality to be on local TV. (I should know!) It's local, and most of these stations are only available online, via podcasts. Draft a brief memo for radio or TV programmers, and modify it as needed:

"I'm a local counselor who works with kids, families, and individuals on issues related to substance abuse, and I'm also a hypnotherapist and life coach. I know your station addresses a lot of community issues, and I would love to be a guest on one of your programs to discuss ways people can improve themselves or work through issues."

It is also advisable to create video content for your website and YouTube. Record your workshops and presentations, and post them on YouTube, Facebook, your website, and any and all media you have access to. You can present a workshop to an empty room and record the content. This is great practice and gives you material to post online. When you review the video, you will see many things that need to be improved, such as stance, wording, and gestures. It can be a rude awakening to see yourself on video, but it will force you to improve.

A ninety-minute workshop can be edited to a thirty- to forty-five-second piece and another edited portion that is two to three minutes long. Feature these on your website and YouTube channel, and follow up with posts on Twitter, Facebook, Instagram, and so on. You can also make entire workshops available upon request for free (digitally).

When people see these excerpts and the "entire workshop available upon request" notice, they infer that you are popular and in demand.

Staying Relevant

Being current on local news, national news, topical magazines, and popular TV and radio is a must. You don't have to enjoy them, nor should you pretend to (nor should you enjoy much of them at all), but you should be aware of what is happening locally, nationally, and internationally. You must have your finger on the pulse of the population. We cannot understand or have insight into humanity if we live in a cave and do not interact with it. You need to know about current trends, past trends, and potential future ones. You never know when you may be able to make an insightful reference or comparison. Which celebrity was arrested this week? What scandal is currently happening in the NFL? How is your local team doing? Know the basics to stay topical and relevant. Know a little about everything.

It makes no difference whether you love reality shows or detest them. They are a part of the culture you are trying to be of service to, so you are required to know of them and how they may influence society—good or bad. It is embarrassing if the people who entrust you to guide them are aware of more than you are.

You do not have to be an expert on any social topic, but you should be minimally informed. This is staying *relevant*.

The "Polymathy" section provides instructions on being relevant and knowledgeable.

Study physics, anthropology, history, science, religion, philosophy, and every cerebral subject you come across. The bigger your body of knowledge, the wider the spectrum of knowledge and insights you have to draw from. My interest in quantum physics rarely comes up in a conversation, yet I use it as an internal frame of reference for a myriad of topics, issues, and subjects. You do not have to quote chapter and verse of any philosophy or religion, but by fusing these concepts into your psyche, you gain access to areas of thought that exist beyond you. These explorations will add layers to your thoughts and texture to your being. The more well rounded you are, the more respected and credible you will be. And the more respected and credible you are, the more your advice will be followed and the more change you will facilitate.

To be a versatile conversationalist, you need to have *basic* knowledge on nearly every relevant topic and have specific, thorough knowledge on a few. You don't need to be the smartest person on the planet, but when counseling, you need to try to be the smartest person in the room. This means knowing a little about nearly everything and a whole lot about a few things.

You are a mentor to your clients, taking on something of a parental role, and mentors are leaders. To guide your clients properly, versatility is vital. Being well informed and well rounded is another way to honor your role, respect your profession, and remain ready to help in as many areas as possible.

Be involved with at least one book, magazine article, or both at all times. Whenever you're asked what you're reading, you should have an answer. We all have useable time—in the toilet, in the line at the DMV, in a waiting room—and if you carry a magazine or a book with you at all times, you will read often and digest volumes of information over time. The more you know, the more you can teach.

The Holy Grail of Private Practice: The Waiting List

Once you attain a waiting list of clients, you've arrived! If you've got a waiting list of people to see you, your practice is successful. Once you've achieved this, you can run fewer workshops and occasionally omit an ad and focus nearly all your time on session work. I do not advise having an actual waiting list. If a client cannot come to a time I have available during the week, I offer to see him or her on the weekend, including Sunday, if that is the only time we can arrange without my bumping someone else.

Personally, I cannot in good conscience refuse to see people because "my schedule is full," which is why I work ten-hour days, six days a week. Whom am I going to tell, "Sorry, I wish I could help you with your crisis and all, but I'm really busy"? No one. I can't. People reach out for help, and if I can help, it seems wrong to say no.

Being a counselor is about much more than financial success or personal fulfillment and validation. It is a duty, and once you accept the responsibility of it, you belong to humanity as much as you belong to yourself or your own family. If you do not want this responsibility, this may not be the best career choice. In the beginning of your practice, you may need to work evenings and weekends to make ends meet, as the small number of clients you have will be spread out at different times and days, and their schedules will not line up with other appointments you have. If you are a millionaire and doing this for fun, I suppose you can afford to be selective about whom you see and when. Until then, see clients when they can see you. Once you are fully established and have the waiting-list status, you can tell clients when you're available and when you're not. Until then, work weekends, evenings, your birthday, major holidays, and any day that ends in *y*. Get it?

I have clients I care a lot about, and their life circumstances can change and make them able to see me only on a Sunday morning or a Friday evening. As mentioned earlier, counseling is not a job of convenience. It is a career, and careers require full—not partial, but full—commitment.

No one creates a successful career without total commitment and sacrifice. Your local doctor may not work weekends and may take vacations and not be available in the evenings, but that doctor put in nonstop days and hours back in graduate school and interned and sacrificed much to achieve that comfort of private-practice success.

Pay your dues now, and reap the benefits later.

I've been waiting-list successful for seven years, and I still work on Sundays and evenings if a client is in crisis and that is the only time we can meet. I don't do it because I'm a workaholic; I do it because my role is not something I can take and leave when it's convenient.

You don't have to be the smartest. You don't have to work harder than everyone else. You do need to be pretty smart and work harder than most everyone else. If you are and you do, the waiting list will be yours someday.

Below are copies of several of my advertorials. The format was four hundred words maximum.

THE SECRET LANGUAGE OF TWEENS, TEENS, AND PRETEENS
MOTIVATING, GETTING RESPECT, AND SETTING BOUNDARIES YOUR KIDS WILL FOLLOW

It feels a lot like you're banging your head against a brick wall, doesn't it? You tell your kids what's right and what's good for them, and they not only ignore you, but they roll their eyes or, worse, become defiant or disrespectful, like you're stupid. It makes you want to give up sometimes, and it seems hopelessly frustrating.

Believe it or not, your kids want you to set boundaries and motivate them. But it is their nature to resist you. Rule number one is to stay calm and not take their behavior personally.

So if they want us to be involved and set rules and motivate them, why are they making it so hard to do? It's how we do it that counts. If we don't learn to speak the right language, we'll never get anywhere. There is a delicate balance that must be adhered to, an ebb and flow of moving in and backing off that gets the best results. When we learn to truly listen and change our language to something that is less critical to them, they begin to respect us. I know how unfair it is that you should have to earn their respect, but it is a fact of life. It's best to accept this fact and learn how to do it properly.

Rule number two: Learn how to advise and discuss and avoid demanding and instructing.

Rule number three: Be the parent, and navigate through conflict.

It's easy to think you're doing it right when you're not. Parents are super busy and often act (or react) on instinct. But if you are facing conflict and disrespect, then there are things you can do better to get results. Rule number four: Don't blame yourself. Kids and culture have changed; nobody gave you the new handbook. Yet.

Reaching out and getting trained in these techniques can provide the missing link. Getting involved with support groups and workshops can be total game changers! Rule number five: Never think you know it all, and don't give up!

Scott Spackey offers private counseling and coaching for families and kids of all ages. A special workshop—Finding the Balance Between "Helicopter" and "Free-Range" Parenting, with two opportunities to attend: Thursday, May 23, at 7:30 p.m. and Saturday, May 25, at 3:00 p.m. Registration is $15. For details: 661-904-3333, Scott@Life-Mind.com, or www.Life-Mind.com.

DRUGS AND INTERVENTION

What do you do if you or someone you love has a drinking or drug problem? Dealing with addiction is complicated, even for trained professionals. Too often, family members feel they can contain the situation, but typically the behavior only spins further out of control.

As any recovering addict will tell you, it is rarely a one-person job to achieve abstinence or sobriety. The underlying issues that contribute to addiction are like a minefield for the untrained person. Not only is there an urgency to getting abuse under control, but underlying psychological issues also need to be addressed. If they're not, relapse is bound to occur. The bottom line: quitting drugs and alcohol is one of the most challenging and painfully difficult experiences a family can endure.

Only 12 percent of addicts who try to quit on their own succeed, compared to 75 percent who seek outside help. There is a lot of help available since addiction exists in every area of society—among the wealthy and poor and across racial boundaries. Valuable years of someone's life can be lost to addiction, years that could have been productive and secure.

The type of help available ranges from self-help like AA and NA to inpatient treatment facilities. AA and NA are successful at providing support so long as someone keeps with the fellowship. Inpatient treatment is an option that can be costly and sometimes impossible due to work and family responsibilities. In the middle is outpatient treatment. Private outpatient treatment allows someone to continue to live while recovering and provides the professional training and customized help the addict needs that is not available in self-help support groups.

This type of counseling is private and discreet, can involve the family, and guides everyone through the issue, including ways to prevent relapse and even facilitate interventions. Interventions are an important step in the recovery process and sometimes mean the difference between life and death. However, it is unwise to perform an intervention without first consulting a professional.

Addiction needs to be looked upon as a disorder. And when someone has a disorder, he or she needs professional help to get well. Addicts who don't get help could lose the best years of their lives and maybe lose their lives altogether. Addiction, no matter what stage it is in, should never be underestimated.

Scott Spackey is a California Registered Addiction Specialist, Interventionist, Certified Clinical Hypnotherapist & Life Coach. 661-299-1999, Scott@Life-Mind.com

DRUG- AND FAMILY-COUNSELING OPTIONS

There are a lot of choices for getting help. Many expensive outpatient and inpatient recovery centers offer little more than prefab formulas and stylized babysitting for those who truly need to be helped before they are lost forever to the disease of addiction. One-size-fits-all recovery programs don't work. Addicts need personal care, customized treatment, and a counselor who cares more about the addict than about corporate policies, TV ratings, and upper-management bonuses and salaries.

Addicts are fragile, vulnerable, and in the middle of a crisis. Just as a mountain climber needs a guide to climb Mount Everest, an addict needs an experienced and trained guide to lead him or her through the process of recovery. Addicts should never try to do it on their own; there is always help available.

Certainly not all treatment centers are bad, but I hope the public will continue to scrutinize carefully when considering treatment for their loved ones. The treatment industry is highly profit driven, and grassroots counselors who are doing the heavy lifting are underpaid despite their tremendous responsibility. This attracts some less-than-qualified individuals who lack the level of insight a complicated person needs.

So what type of treatment is best?

Treatment facilities are expensive, and there's a major downside: when you put a bunch of addicts together, bad things can happen. Addicts joke that one of the easiest place to score drugs is rehab. Patients who are not trying to stay clean mix with those who are.

A combination of counseling, group support, and family support is usually best. Twelve-step meetings are free and always around. They have a well-thought-out program for sobriety; however, they are still a support group and lack training and objectivity. Many of today's youth do not resonate with AA. Rehab and AA boast a success rate lower than 8 percent.

Private counseling is discreet, customized, and personal. One-on-one guidance is effective and safe, and it gets results. The best strategies are customized to the individual; the way he or she thinks and feels is unique, and the path to recovery needs to be equally unique. Don't lose someone to addiction. It is never too early to get someone help if he or she is using, but it can be too late.

Scott Spackey is a registered addiction specialist, interventionist, life coach, and hypnotherapist. www.LIFE-MIND.com   Scott@Life-Mind.com   661-904-3333

Marketing

20

"Let me comment on something we talked about earlier before we're out of time..."

Each section of this book is intentional and purposeful, not gratuitous. Some of the topics and instructions may seem elementary to you, and others may be recommendations you may not have thought of on your own. The selections that seem elementary to you may be elusive to some candidates, and vice versa. There are even people out there who would find this entire manual elementary, but if you've read this far, you must be finding things that are useful.

As I mentioned in "What I Did" regarding my contracting start-up, many books and schools skip over things that they often assume are elementary. HMI presented material on marketing, and it was very useful information even though I already knew most of what was presented from having run my own business for eight years already.

Almost the entire curriculum of my drug-counselor education was basic to me due to my prolific history with drugs and addicts and my penchant for reading. What those schools teach is vital to know and must be included since there is a percentage of students who are ignorant to some of the information.

This book was written with that assumption in mind—that the reader knows absolutely nothing about beginning a private practice.

It is my dream to encourage and empower intelligent people who are enthusiastic about making a difference. More valuable than institutional education is insight, instinct, and passion. Truly passionate motivation creates a clarity no education can provide. If a person has all of them—instincts, passion, *and* effective education—he or she can create a powerful practice and save many people from self-destruction.

The devotion, dedication and appreciation my clients have graced me with, is such a powerful force that it resurrected me from near death. When I was dying in the hospital, these people visited me, prayed for me, and begged for my life. I thought I had a made a good business and was grateful to have such a successful practice, but I'd never had time to truly consider what difference, if any, I had truly made to those I had worked for. I always tried to serve them, for I felt they deserved quality help and my sincerest effort, and I certainly tried, each and every day, to serve them well. But I was completely unaware of the impact I had made on so many lives until so many people returned to see me for counsel even though I could barely walk or talk yet. They trusted me to pull through and to figure out how to advise them. My recovery was the result of their demand: They told me they would not be well without me in their lives and that I needed to live and not abandon them. I am honored to have made such a difference to people.

This book is dedicated to those who would not allow me to be excused from work. This book is dedicated to those I've yet to advise. This book is dedicated to those whom *you* will advise. Not you, not me, but them. Those who need assistance, answers, and guidance. Those who permit us to serve. They give us the opportunity to have a fulfilling career, not just a job.

I want to create an army. An army of counselors who provide custom, well-crafted, and meaningful guidance. A gentle army. A force of healing and sensibility.

Contrary to popular belief, I do not wish for the dismantling of the conventional helping processes or rehab recovery. I want the new to coexist with the old: the existing recovery industry should be an alternative, not the only option. I do not want the private-practice recovery field to become the only option, either. Both have their role in the field of counseling and recovery, and the time for the private-practice option to emerge is now.

By enhancing each other, they will serve humanity more effectively, without the driving force being the politics and bottom-line revenue. Policy and revenue are vital, but they do not need to come at the expense of authenticity. It may be just crazy enough to be true that we can put quality first and make a stellar profit, too. Don't sacrifice your ideals to succeed: compromise them. There's a huge difference. To sacrifice is to sell or trade your ideals. To compromise is to sensibly adapt them to the machinery of the world while sustaining their essence.

Make a difference.

One person at a time.

One session at a time.

Put your messages, ideals, methods, and values in a nice package that looks good on the outside and is something the public can digest. But keep the content of the package honest. The truth is often not pretty or easy to look at, but if it's packaged properly, it will be surprisingly well accepted. Don't sacrifice the content: keep the content authentic and true, but dress it up. Your appearance, your office, your cards, your workshops—the package should be tuxedos and evening gowns, but the content within needs to be the real thing, raw and honest.

Yes, you can do both, You can succeed without the university education, have real income and a comfortable life and nice things, and provide a service you can be proud of, all the while being certain that you have made truth and honesty the priority.

The Author

Scott Spackey was involved with a notorious Los Angeles organized counterfeit and methamphetamine ring in the 90's.

He left home just after he turned 16, living wherever he could. He started with pot at 13, regularly dosing LSD by 15 and shooting-up heroin, cocaine and meth at 17. Scott is a poly-drug addict, having abused every drug accessible, including one that is unknown beyond a secretive drug culture of addicts, gangsters and organized criminals. Grand theft auto, robbery, cheater, liar and dope fiend were his calling cards. Most of his associates are either dead, in prison or still on drugs, yet he somehow survived and is going on over twenty years being clean.

Scott provides keynote speeches at recovery conventions, provides workshops, authors several books, is a monthly contributor to a Los Angeles magazine and has appeared on Los Angeles TV and radio. He mentors and trains other addiction counselors and still maintains his private practice. His memoir, A Stone's Throw, Memoir of a Dope Fiend, is in the beginning stages of film development.

He lives in Southern California near his girlfriend of 12 years and his 22 year old son. He was born June 28, 1966.

He travels the world for adventure, having been to 12 different countries, including 5 spiritual pilgrimages to India. He rarely travels the landmark sites, preferring the road far less traveled. He travels to expand the boundaries of his own consciousness and character.

He is currently working on his sequel memoir, Throwing Stones and a series of guide books on world religions and Eastern philosophies. In 2013 he was hit by another driver while on his motorcycle. He died instantly but was revived by paramedics, having to learn to walk and talk from scratch he is documenting his challenges in another memoir in an attempt to help others with similar tragedy.

BOOKS FROM
PRIMORDIAL PRODUCTIONS

Project Addiction
The Complete Guide to Using, Abusing and
Recovering from Drugs and Behaviors
476 Pages, 7.5x9.25 inches (24 Illustrations,
Warning, Help resources)

ISBN: 978-0-9968913-0-1 (paperbound) $23.99
ISBN: 978-0-9968913-4-9 (Audio) - $29.99
ISBN: (ePUB) 978-0-9968913-3-2- $9.99

A Stone's Throw—Memoir of a Dope Fiend
By Scott Spackey
273 Pages, 8.5x11 inches (4 Illustrations)

ISBN: 978-0-9968913-2-5 (paperbound) $21.99
ISBN: 978-0-9968913-8-7 (Audio) - $23.99
ISBN: 978-0-9968913-7-0 (ePUB) - $9.99

All books available from your favorite book
dealer or
from the publisher:
www.PrimordialProductions.net

To contact the Publisher:
CCB@PrimordialProductions.net

To contact the Author:
Scott@ProjectAddictionCounselor.net

SALES & CONTACT

Additional copies of
Project Addiction Counselor—How to Create and
Sustain a Private Practice
are available through your favorite
book dealer or from the publisher:

Primordial Productions
24303 Walnut St., Suite A
Valencia, CA 91321
Phone: 661.383.3182
Website: www.PrimordialProductions.net
E-mail: CCB@PrimordialProductions.net

Project Addiction Counselor
ISBN (Print version): 978-0692387931 $12.95
(ePUB version):978-0-9968913-9-4 $9.99
(Audio version): 978-0-9968913-8-7 $18.99

To contact Scott Spackey:
E-mail: Scott@ProjectAddictionCounselor.net

Made in the USA
Columbia, SC
03 September 2018